"Regina Lynn is a true sex-tech explorer. If you own a computer, surf the web, or like sex, you should definitely read this book."

—Jamye Waxman, columnist, *Playgirl Magazine*

"It's about time someone reported back on the pleasures and perils of sex on the internet. Regina Lynn has the experience and talent to make things understandable even to the biggest newbie."

—Tom Merritt, editor, CNET.com

"Regina Lynn's take on personal relationships within online gaming communities is both insightful and stimulating."

—Todd White, writer/producer, G4TV

The Sexual Revolution 2.0

Getting Connected, Upgrading Your Sex Life,
and Finding True Love—or at Least a Dinner Date—
in the Internet Age

REGINA LYNN

Ulysses Press

Published by: Ulysses Press
P.O. Box 3440
Berkeley, CA 94703
www.ulyssespress.com

Library of Congress Control Number: 2005922420
ISBN 1-56975-477-2

Printed in Canada by Transcontinental Printing

10 9 8 7 6 5 4 3 2 1

Editorial and production staff: Ashley Chase, Steven Schwartz, Claire Chun, Matt Orendorff
Cover design: Robles-Aragón

Distributed by Publishers Group West

To the Sex Drive forum

Contents

Acknowledgements

Thank you to Kelli and Kathryn for your tireless research on my behalf, especially since I know it involves more libraries, internet searches and phone calls than sex.

Thank you to Janine, Big Dave, Bev and Mary for the mentoring, the pep talks and the haven in which to speak freely.

Thank you to Mom and Dad for the support—emotional, professional, and emergency financial—that kept me going when I didn't think I would make it.

Thank you to Janet for allowing me the flexibility to pursue my dreams without giving up my day job.

Thank you to Wired News for setting such high standards for Sex Drive.

Thank you to Ulysses Press for my editor Ashley, my copyeditor Beverly and my publicist Sara. Every author hopes for the kind of patience and guidance you have given me, and I know how lucky I am to have it.

Thank you most especially to Whitney, Seth and Patricia. If I wrote out all the reasons why, this book would be twice as long. Also, you would all be mortified.

And thank you to Clay. Who knew?

I've always known it takes a village to birth a book, and I give thanks every day that my village has no idiots. Any erroneous assumptions about technology or relationships that may have made it into the final version of this book are entirely my fault, even if I'd like to blame them on the internet.

Manifesto

What is the sexual revolution 2.0? It's sex and the internet, sex and science, sex and communication. It's the sex of technology and the technology of sex, two of the most powerful forces at work in our modern lives—and it's the foundation of a social revolution.

My weekly online column, "Sex Drive," examines the newest sexual revolution from a perspective not shared by mainstream media. For more than two years, first at TechTV and then at Wired News, readers have expected Sex Drive to comment on techno-sexual trends, to challenge the status quo, and to highlight technologies developing today that will improve our sex lives tomorrow.

I love writing Sex Drive. I tell people it is where sex and tech come together, and while that may sound flippant, it's amazing just how true the pun has become. The Digital Age, the Information Economy, whatever you want to call it, is an eloquent expression of humankind's need to create, to build, to imagine and invent. Sex, the ultimate creative act, is a silly, joyful, exploited, loving, crazy, transcendent, downright ridiculous and sometimes even eloquent expression of humankind's need to connect. The column and this book are the results of 10 years of immersing myself in both, geeking out and exploring the depths of my sexuality, often at the same time.

Sometimes the union of sex and technology is seamless, effortless, perfect. Other times, the combination has as much subtlety as Ouchy the Clown at a ladies' auxiliary quilting circle and Bible hour. But there's no denying that technology has changed, is changing, and will continue to change how humans experience sexual and romantic relationships.

Including yours.

You might not be aware of how often technology touches your sex life. Many of us use technology to exert control over reproduction, which, last I checked, was related to sex (although maybe not for much longer). Maybe you use technology to write email to your lover(s) every day; you might have gotten yourself into trouble with a Freudian send, directing an erotic missive to a boss and a project update to a prospective date. You or someone you know has loved and lost through the internet. An entire generation is flirting by SMS, writing in abbreviations invented by and for the under-21 set.

Vibrators are coming (back) out of the closet, along with a host of accoutrements, including a way to connect them to the internet so someone else can adjust their speeds and intensities for you. And cybersex is alive and well in the internet underground, protected from newbies and spam by virtual moats. (I know, because I accidentally stepped in one and got my toes nipped by the dragon when I linked to a particular website from my column. The owner of the site was not pleased by the flood of visitors he got that week. Oops.) And almost everyone has looked at online porn. Don't pretend you haven't.

If you've ever been embarrassed or ashamed of how you've used tech in your sexual experiences, don't be. (Well, unless they were truly shameful activities, in which case, *get help*.) You're not the only person who's done what you've done. Even if I haven't gone there too, you can bet your bottom that somebody has. And it's probably online, available to anyone with a few bucks and a credit card.

This book might make you uncomfortable. It might make you laugh. It might even turn you on. I'm not holding back about the things I've done—you'll know that I know whereof I speak. (Mom, please refer to my list of sections you aren't allowed to read, which I have sent to you by email. Thanks.)

Because I've experienced much of what I write about. I'm not locked in a turret atop a tower, ivory or otherwise. Cybersex, online dating, connecting with lovers across the country—I've sampled them all. I've even fallen in love in cyberspace, twice. Once was a standard six-month whirlwind that took place purely online. The other evolved into a real-world relationship measured in years, not months. I've forged friendships online that expanded to offline, I've lived solo while feeling more connected to the world than ever before, and most recently I've incorporated various technologies into my relationship with a lover who manages to surprise and delight me more each day.

I'm no stranger to teledildonics, either.

Humans have always sought to sexualize technology and to technologize sex. As author Annalee Newitz says, humans are a tool-oriented species, however far back you go. So why would anyone think it strange that we bring technology into the bedroom (or the shower, onto the kitchen table or the living room rug—you get the idea)?

Robert Heinlein is credited with the observation that "progress doesn't come from early risers—progress is made by lazy people looking for easier ways to do things," and to some extent that's true. I would also add that progress is made by people looking for more ways to explore, expand and enjoy the sexual variety scientists claim only humans, of all Earth's creatures, can achieve.

I've done my best to chart this sexual revolution to date, and look at where I think we're going, based on my experiences, observations, and research. But like any massive cultural change, the entire phenomenon can't fit into one book. My intention is not to chronicle every moment, every internet-inspired climax or every technology involved, but to start the dialog.

My conversations with thousands of Sex Drive readers are the best part of my job and the main impetus behind this book. I want to provoke you to think and talk about the revolution, even as we create it. Only by paying attention can we avoid the traps and fears so many have already written about. I want you to come away from this book with something to say, and I invite you to come to reginalynn.com to say it.

Because, and I know this is hard to believe, it's not all about me. The internet—and, coincidentally, sex—is all about connection. I owe a big thanks to all the folks who generously shared their stories, insights and time with me. You know who you are.

It's only the beginning. I'm looking forward to all that the sexual revolution 2.0 has to offer, and I hope when you've finished reading this book, talking about it with your friends and passing it around at parties, you will be too.

See you on the other side,

Regina Lynn
Los Angeles
June 2005
reginalynn.com

1

Email and Instant Message: In the Beginning Was the Word

In the movie *Dead Poets Society*, Robin Williams as Mr. Keating tells his students that "language was developed for one endeavor." In the significant pause that follows, he lets his gaze roam from boy to boy, waiting for them to answer just what endeavor he means. Finally, one of the boys asks in an uncertain voice, "To communicate?" Mr. Keating shakes his head. "No!" he cries. "To woo women!"

If language was created to woo women, the internet was created to woo more women (and men) more often. Forget what they told you about defense departments and universities. The internet has done more to help us upgrade our sex lives than any other technology in history—including the printing press, the telegraph, the home movie camera and the DVD player. And while the spectacular inventions like teledildonics and robotic love dolls grab the headlines and titillate the imagination, it's the pedestrian internet applications that are the true heart of the sexual revolution 2.0.

The majority of Americans are online now, and that's not all urbanites. According to Pew Internet Research, even in rural areas more than half of Americans were using the internet by 2004. Other developed countries show similar trends. And we're incorporating the internet into our personal lives in greater and greater numbers.

That's no surprise—it's no secret that sex is one of the primary drivers of technological innovation, and we eventually assimilate every new communications technology into our relationships. It wasn't uncommon for telegraph operators to fall in love over the wires, even though they had to do it through Morse code. And it's not only more common, it's becoming more socially acceptable to court and even fall in love online, whether you first meet on the internet or in person.

Young couples today—and quite a few old ones—would no more conduct a relationship without the internet than they would without telephones and cars. The sexual revolution 2.0 is creating the *expectation* that lovers will email each other, for better or for worse. Everyone knows the foundation of a good relationship is good communication. What is the most universal function of a personal computer? No, not porn. Your PC exists to capture, format and deliver words to and from people. Everything else rests on top of that single, essential function.

Bare Yourself, Virtually

We are often more naked in our writing than we are in person, more apt to divulge secrets and "go deep." And we do it a lot sooner online than we do in real life. People will write to me after reading one of my columns and tell me the most intimate details of their relationships, such as their sexual fantasies or a technique they have developed to work around a physical disability. I've had readers ask me questions about erectile difficulties, solicit my advice on their sex toy purchases, and reveal their deepest fears about sex. One widowed man wondered if cybersex would help him "move on"—it had been three years since his wife had died, and he was feeling pressured by friends to "get out there again."

Readers brought up all of these personal, intimate subjects in their first contacts with me. They felt comfortable talking about these subjects in email with someone they had never met but with whom they felt a connection. In our correspondence I found most of them to be intelligent, thoughtful people. I doubt any of them would have introduced themselves to me at a party, no matter how well they thought they knew me through my column, with "Hi, I'm Dave, and I feel like I'm competing with my wife's vibrator—but I can't compete." They also would not have bothered to write if they had to commit their thoughts to paper, stick it in an envelope, find a stamp and put it in the mail. Snail mail gives you too many chances to change your mind. With email, once you've clicked Send, there's very little you can do.

There's something comforting about knowing another human is reading your words, validating your fears or swooning over your seductive siren song—yet not facing you across a table in a crowded Starbucks. In some ways, starting an email relationship can be a lot like starting a journal, except that the journal writes back. One Sex Drive reader says:

> [Email] allows for honest interaction
> that can't go on in many community or work-
> place watering holes. It opens up opportuni-

ties for personal expression that may otherwise have been denied. There are three taboo
subjects in many social settings: sex, religion and politics. Other subjects that usually don't fit in the mainstream are things
such as the arts and sciences unless one
works in a related field. It's always easier
to talk about interests when they are shared.
Even when there are conflicting opinions on
a matter.

Email communication can create a sense of intimacy, real or false, that carries into your real-world interaction. It is redefining our expectations of how we get to know each other and how we sustain a relationship. After you experience the perceived and actual closeness that can develop over email, you will probably feel that something is missing when you have a relationship without an email component. And if you then get involved with someone who hates email, issues of connectedness and distance can well up and cause problems (as you'll see in the next chapter).

As Dave Barry would say, I am not making this up. I'm not the only one who values email in all types of relationships, from friendship to flirtation to forever, to the point where if there's no email, there's almost no relationship at all. In their chapter of the *2004 Annual Psychology Review*, "The Internet and Social Life," psychologists John A. Bargh and Katelyn Y.A. McKenna write about a 1995 study that concluded "online relationships are highly similar to those developed in person in terms of their breadth, depth and quality." That was 10 years ago, the very beginning of the sexual revolution 2.0, and already sociologists and psychologists recognized that the relationships we forged online were not a fad or mere shadow relationships.

Another study, performed in 2002, found that more than half of the respondents who started close relationships in online discussion groups ended up meeting face to face; 22 percent "reported that they had either married, became engaged to, or were living with someone they initially met on the internet."

These studies focused on people who participated in "randomly selected popular newsgroups" organized around everyday topics like fashion, health and politics. If the studies included sex-oriented newsgroups, Bargh and McKenna don't mention them. One can easily extrapolate that members of sexual forums are more likely to form sexual relationships with each other, at least online, than members of my roommate's mother's online recipe club.

The most significant findings in these studies, in the context of the sexual revolution 2.0, are twofold. For one thing, the real-world couples who first met online were as stable two years later as couples who met and courted in a more traditional manner. For another, people felt they were better able to express their true selves—which Bargh and McKenna define as "those self-aspects they felt were important but which they were usually unable to present in public"—when they met online than they were when they met in person.

This is an almost entirely new phenomenon for human beings. No snail-mail penpal relationship can develop as fast or as absorbingly as email relationships. When hours or minutes—rather than days or weeks—pass between letters, hearts respond. It's no wonder we're confused about whether falling in love over email is "legitimate;" whether exchanging erotic fantasies with someone you've never met is weird; whether emailing with a woman for a year counts as having "met" her, even if all of your interaction has been by internet and phone. Yet, in the context of human sexual evolution, email has been around for a mere sneeze. We can't expect to have all the answers so soon. We've only just begun to ask the questions.

A Sex Drive reader said it well:

> It's funny how it's easier to be more honest and openhearted online. The anonymity of the internet allows you to truly be yourself, while the same kind of openness in your favorite local pub or bar can be the source of gossip and ridicule for the rest of your life, especially if you live in a small community.

Almost everyone I talk to has some sort of personal story about a close connection by email. Bargh and McKenna report that internet partners who liked each other projected qualities of their ideal friends onto each other, which led to feelings of closeness, as did the "relative anonymity of the internet ... reducing the risks inherent in self-disclosure." So even if you've never written a letter in your life, if you get to talking online, you will go places you probably wouldn't—or couldn't—in any other venue.

In her book *How to Write a Dirty Story*, sex educator Susie Bright says:

> Writing as a team, side by side--where you exchange sentences, pages, and concepts, fashioning a work together--is an incredible aphrodisiac. If your results are any good at all, you're going to be attracted to each other. It's competitive, yes, but also thrilling. There's no statistical survey to prove my point, but I defy any writing team to tell me they haven't felt the tug and consequences of the heat they create together.

That holds true whether you're writing a book or a two-paragraph email to someone you hope to sleep with someday. Try it. I dare you.

Love Connections

Because of email, more people are writing more letters than at any time throughout history. How many letters did you send in a week before you had email? On how many days did you send more than one letter? And how many emails did you send and receive yesterday?

Years ago I read an article about the "lost art" of letter-writing. Email had replaced handwritten epistles, the writer bemoaned, leading to a demise of manners, consideration and caring; the underlying assumption was that ink on fine stationery was a superior form of communication, and the longer it took to craft a letter, the more the sender cared about the recipient. I've even received email to this effect from Sex Drive readers who were offended that I suggested that email is an essential part of modern relationships.

Horsefeathers. Nothing seizes a netizen's attention better than a well-crafted email, sparkling with wit and personality, enticing the recipient to return again and again to the mailbox for the pleasure of re-reading it. Or better yet, the possibility of having received another email *that very same day*.

Email removes all excuses. You can't blame a busy job or a hectic schedule for your inattentiveness, not when you can literally write a brief-but-sincere love letter in 30 seconds. Given more time, you can craft an epistle that rivals the best Cyrano ever composed for Roxanne. It may not be as verbose, as educated or as French, but as long as it's honest, it will produce the same heart flutters. Hidden among the volume of chatty, everyday gossip and stupid jokes are some of the most beautiful love letters ever written. I know, because I've received some. With no excuse for being inattentive, why not attend instead? Talk about a clue that he (or she) *is* just that into you!

One Sex Drive reader wrote to tell me he had sent his wife a love note from work—using a personal email account—after reading one of my columns. From what I understand, she liked it. A lot.

Most employers have rules against using company resources for personal activities, but I'm not suggesting that you send a *Penthouse*-style "I never believed these stories were true, but ... " letter using the corporate Microsoft Exchange server. I think employers should encourage us to take a minute here and there to log onto a webmail account and send our beloveds a quick reminder of our undying desire and affection. A happy, fulfilling home life bodes well for our performance on the job, and permitting judicious use of webmail on company time strikes me as sound corporate policy.

Just remember that your network administrator has to monitor the network for a variety of legitimate reasons, which means that nothing on your computer is entirely secret. The IT department has a copy of every email you've sent and received over the company network. Instant messaging is not the answer—IT can view anything on your computer while it's on the network, including your chat logs and the window you have open on your screen. A webmail message may not be intercepted, but that doesn't mean it can't be read while you're composing or reading it. The uber-geeky can increase their chances of privacy by setting up SSH tunnels or encryption (don't keep the encryption key on the office PC!), but how many of us can or want to do that?

Speaking of geeky. I've always wondered whether other people liked the tactile nature of email—feeling each key, backspacing to get your words just right—or if that was just my own personal fetish. I replace every straight keyboard with a curved one and have a particular affinity for the Logitech ergonomic wireless keyboard (although I hate the accompanying mouse). But even if you don't have a thing for keyboard responsiveness and curves, email can still turn you on.

Email—done right—can be foreplay. In fact, it can almost be sex. Women who would never admit to looking at pornographic pictures can be aroused by written erotica, particularly stories created just for them, centered around their pleasure. Men who had no idea that women have well-developed sexual imaginations can be surprised by the sheer detail a woman often includes in her side of the conversation. I'm not talking about lists of actions you'd like to do to each other. I'm talking about real, honest sexual imagery that takes into account all the senses as well as your favorite verbs.

Men who are too shy to approach a woman at a social gathering, and women who feel uncomfortable making the first move in person, often discover a latent ability to flirt and seduce by email. One friend of mine carried on a love relationship over email for almost a year before he felt comfortable enough to pick up the phone. It was another two years before they met in person. From what I hear (from them and from their neighbors), it was worth the wait.

Chat up a woman in a bar and you're as likely to get her email address—an auxiliary account she uses only for such occasions—as her phone number. (If this isn't incentive for single men to hone their email skills, I don't know what is.) For a woman, giving out an email address feels safer than revealing a phone number, so we are more likely to take the chance and give it up.

That works in everyone's favor—not only is it easier to exchange contact information, it gives both parties the chance to start the seduction with the very first word. It expands our chances of meeting a compatible mate; you can't get to know someone as deeply at a bar or a party as you can over email, and those who are too shy to carry on a long conversation at first sight may turn out to be incredible correspondents in email. And then when you go on a first date, the ice is already broken.

Dr. Janet Lever, sociologist at California State University, Los Angeles, has studied office romance as well as online romance. In her research, she has found that many people who would never approach a co-worker in person have done so by email instead, with varying degrees of success. The sense that you are taking less of a risk—if you're rejected, it's probably going to be in the form of a lack of reply or a written "no thanks"—helps you gather the courage to broach the subject. On the other hand, you now have a written record of your attempt to start an office romance, so be careful out there. A delicate touch, whether you're writing to a man or a woman, will get you farther than a heavy hand.

She has also found that email is the great equalizer when it comes to dating. Even today, women of all ages hesitate to make the first move in person or over the phone. Women who might think twice about asking a man out, either from an old-fashioned sense of propriety or a concern about seeming needy, show none of that hesitation in email. A flirtatious email that teases, a slightly

bolder reply, a skillful dance of intention and tens*
by the time you get to a first date you're both pr*
romance.

The Problem With Instant Gratification Is That It's Not Fast Enough

Some people prefer email flirtation because it's asynchronous. You can take as much time as you need to say exactly the right thing, to look up song lyrics and poetry to paste into your letter, to respond to just the parts of your lover's most recent letter that you want to answer. Email lets you exchange monologues, sans interruption, distraction and unwanted tangents. It's an excellent medium for long, rambling musings on the nature of love, sex and the cosmos.

But there's nothing like instant messaging to bring out your true sexual self.

Instant messaging has been a favorite sex toy of mine since 1998 when I began using ICQ, which I believe was the most popular messaging client of the day. Since then I have used IM to have cybersex with strangers and with lovers (more about that in Chapter 3), to flirt with friends and to masturbate, sometimes all at the same time. (I've also used it to communicate with editors and clients, but never at the same time as those other activities. I'm not stupid.)

IM is unmatched in its ability to keep long-distance relationships alive, whether you're apart for a weekend, a week or a year. IM has the nakedness of email and the immediacy of phone contact, without an astronomical phone bill. You also have the intimacy of written communication, and the intellectual involvement of reading not just the other person's words but their intentions as well, without the vocal cues of tone and breath or the visual cues of facial expression and gestures.

For cyber lovers, IM provides a private space where they can combine their imaginations and build an almost purely cerebral relationship. And of course it is the cyber-sex equivalent of a basic motel room—ubiquitous, safe, anonymous and clean.

IM requires lovers to stretch their intuition, to practice patience, to accept that each might misinterpret the other, and to give each other the benefit of the doubt. It's an incredibly intimate experience to co-write an erotic scene in IM, each person contributing a line, flinging the narrative back and forth like a badminton birdie without missing a stroke. Lovers who didn't think they were "good writers" soon realize that typos and misspellings and creative grammar hardly matter, as long as the intelligence, the honesty and the imagination come through. (One caveat—if you're prone to typing in SMS abbreviations, make sure ur pRtnR is hip 2 D lingo 1st.)

Like email, IM can remove the distractions of physical appearance and social awkwardness, connecting people on a deeper, more internal level. Or you can fire up the webcam and bring a touch of real-world visuals into the intercourse. Many instant message programs, even the free ones, have a webcam option so that one or both of you can see the other as you chat.

Not everyone is comfortable with IM, and some people have no interest in becoming so. Yet IM has become a "killer app," driving the popularity of mobile devices like Sidekicks and Blackberries. You can install IM on many handhelds and PDAs; I use Agile Messenger on my Dell Axim x30 handheld so I can chat with people on several platforms, including AIM, MSN, Yahoo, ICQ and IRC. Not bad for a device that fits into an evening bag.

Even couples who live together use IM in their daily communications. I use it with my roommate to avoid shouting up and down the stairs, although there's nothing sexual in our relationship. If you live in a multi-computer household, you probably already know how convenient IM can be. You can chat with your lover while you do other things, like banking online or outlining a business proposal. Even some workplaces have relented, risking the distraction factor in order to take advantage of the productivity benefits of IM (and if you're IM-oriented, there are many).

I suspect that any workplace that uses IM as a productivity tool has also seen IM used for mild or even overt flirtation among coworkers. There's something about IM that just seems bring out our naughty sides. Perhaps it's because flirting is only one step beyond telling jokes.

IM is almost as universal as email, but its role in the sexual revolution 2.0 is more visible, perhaps because it is either reviled or loved—few people are in the middle when it comes to IM. Among young people, IM is more popular than email. According to Pew Research, by fall 2004, 42 percent of Americans who used the internet also used instant messaging. That's 52 *million* people.

A poll of the Sex Drive forum revealed that when a person is going to spend a romantic evening alone with a technology, it's most likely going to be instant messaging (with and without webcam). IM even won out over the Sinulator, which might surprise you after you read the Cybersex chapter. True, this was a non-scientific, utterly self-selected survey, but it reflects the trend I have explored in two years of writing the column. Technology is merely a means to an end, not an end in itself. And that end is to connect with other people.

The Freudian Send

One danger that lurks in this new realm of e-lating is that our words will be read by the one person who should not see them. The Freudian send—where you write an email about person A that you intend to send to person B but accidentally send to person A—takes only a second to commit, but the fallout can last a lifetime. It happens when you're so obsessed with the person under fire that you type his name into the To: box. Sometimes it's more insidious: You forget to check the CC: field; you "reply to all" or to a mailing list; or you simply click the wrong button.

My email program automatically fills in an address when I type a few characters. I have to be careful not to send Pat's mail to Patricia, and after my first Freudian send I taught myself to check all of the address fields before clicking Send. For someone who sends as many emails as I do, and who can type and click faster than she can think, well, this is quite an accomplishment.

But you know how it is if you've done it. You're analyzing your relationship or your crush or your ex. Or maybe you're complaining. Or trying to work out how to say something difficult to them in a way that won't hurt their feelings. Or even wanting a friend's input on the script you're planning to use when you dump your partner later next week. You spend extra time explaining your position, revising and rewriting until you're as clear as you know how to be. And then when you're done, often tired or wrung out from the effort, you do the easy part: type their name into the address field and send it off.

Once you've sent it to the wrong person, there's no way out.

When you slip up in your speech, you suffer a few moments of embarrassment. You apologize. Then it's over, forgotten. The recipient of a Freudian send, on the other hand, has your honest, thought-out opinion right there on the screen. You didn't craft your message by accident, you simply sent it to the wrong person. You can't pretend you didn't mean what you said.

An apology is nowhere near adequate.

As one friend of mine put it, after learning that he'd sent his complaint to his girlfriend instead of to his confidant:

```
      She came straight over with a series
of questions that I tap-danced through like
Gregory Hines on double Starbucks. I managed
to recast my "observations" in a more ambigu-
ous (read: less life-threatening) and sophis-
ticated light.
```

Why the Word Matters

Email and instant messaging are becoming the record of our lives. You can search them, print them, save them. You can re-read the phrases that most moved you, as often as you like. (But no fair cutting and pasting these into emails to other lovers—that's cheating.) You can trace entire relationships just by searching your email for a particular name. Your letters, his letters, displayed in order whenever you feel like calling them up. Imagine the archive you'll have after 10 years together. Imagine the transcripts of a lifetime.

One of the greatest advantages of email is that it does not expose all of your deletions and rewrites. Your beloved will not be able to obsess over what you scribbled out in an attempt to decipher what you started to say before you changed your mind. An email is always legible, and it can be read aloud by a computer if the recipient has a visual impairment. Both you and your correspondent can search through the letters archive at any time much more easily than scanning through a stack of paper letters.

Just remember that email captures the thoughts and feelings of a moment and holds them for all time. Angry words spoken in person can be denied or forgotten; vicious email can be revisited for years, intentionally or not, until a technical blessing-in-disguise erases them forever.

We often forget just how much trust we place in those we email. Every epistle leaves us vulnerable to having our privates published, our words forwarded without our permission, our clandestine communication discovered on our own computers by prying eyes. And yet we still email our deepest thoughts and our private fantasies and fears. Email is transforming our sex lives precisely because it already occupies such an ordinary place in our day-to-day life. We think no more of its technological marvels than we think of our telephones, and yet it is an essential part of modern relationships. It has broadened the pool of potential mates, enabling us to interact with like-minded people all over the globe as well as in our own backyards.

The internet medium is new to human experience, but the emotion it helps us feel and express is not. The same challenges and triumphs that have always been a part of sexual attraction still await us. The difference is we have developed a technology that reveals more of our inner selves to one another, for better and for worse. It can help us navigate the perilous waters of love, or it can lure us into the deep end to struggle and drown. I don't care if you've known each other for 50 years or five seconds: email and IM will show new sides of your lover, and of yourself, that you didn't know existed.

But before you run off to fall in love over the internet, remember this caveat. Email may be changing our sex lives—but that doesn't mean it can replace the reality of living together on a daily basis. In the studies cited by Bargh and McKenna, participants reported liking each other more when they first met online than when they first met in person. This sounds like an excellent argument for meeting in person so you can let go some of the idealism and accept yourselves as fallible human beings before making any commitments to move across the country or leave a spouse.

Talking About the Revolution

Come to the forum at www.reginalynn.com and share your thoughts on how the internet affects your relationships.

Have you ever talked with someone online about subjects you would not bring up if you were face-to-face?

Do you have a special email address your partner doesn't know about?

What has sex over IM taught you about your own sexuality, desires and fears? What about your partner's?

REVOLUTIONARY PROFILE
Dr. Janet Lever

Janet Lever, Ph.D., is a sociology professor at California State University, Los Angeles. She conducted the "2004 Cybersex and Romance Survey" for ELLE *magazine and MSNBC.com, as well as previous surveys about body image (2003) and office romance (2002).*

Do men and women have different expectations for the internet in their relationships?

Oh, definitely. Women are using it to learn from other women and realizing that they aren't alone in their feelings. They're really clear about talking about what they see online that stretches their own sexual horizons, things they want to bring back into their personal relationships. For men, often fantasy is fantasy, and has nothing to do with their real relationship.

What did you learn from the cybersex survey that you might not have expected?

When I signed on to do the survey, ELLE was not confident about what would come back, or whether their readers would be interested in participating in a study about erotic sites. Our idea was to include online dating in the survey, so it covered both online personals and erotic sites. That way we doubled our chance that readers would really be involved in the phenomenon. It seemed to me that erotic sites and dating were different topics, with the only common link being they are both done by computer.

But what we quickly came to understand was that the lines were very fuzzy. A lot of people used the dating sites who never wanted to meet anyone—women especially had to learn how to distinguish between guys looking for flirty and dirty talk from the men who wanted to meet. And it turns out that an almost equal number of people met someone through chat rooms. Erotic sites and dating had more in common than I thought. It's not what we anticipated.

What kind of impact is the internet having on relationships? Is it as big as, say, the birth control pill?

It's in the running to be something as big as the Pill. One of the areas where it's having a lot of impact is in who pays for dates, who asks who out. Women initiate emails, even though most women still don't initiate dates in real life. Women feel as free to initiate online as they do to respond. In a bar, women bat their eyes and catch glances, but they don't walk over and introduce themselves. I think the fact that women can be the hunters and the initiators is the kind of thing that does say revolution, a gender revolution.

The Pill leveled the playing field for women, who have always paid a greater price for pregnancy [than men]. The Pill was terrifically important for allowing women to have sex without worrying about reproduction. The internet is doing a similar thing, leveling the playing field. I mean, it's been 35 years [since the sexual revolution], you'd think some of my female students would say they initiate dates, but few of them do. Online, it's 50/50.

To my mind, the internet is really releasing women. Women—everybody—can explore their sexuality now. Men did a damn good job before, through magazines and the like. Areas of fantasy were not hidden to men. Women were much more sheltered; erotic magazines didn't cater to women.

Most women are more oriented to words than to the visual, and now they're learning about sexuality from others' words. And because it's interactive, it's far more powerful than a book or magazine.

2

Mobile Devices: Connectivity Compatibility

In the past few years, people have started having computer sex without the computer. OK, technically speaking, mobile devices like cell phones and Palm Pilots are computers, some more than others. But we're no longer sitting in front of a monitor or snuggled down in bed with a laptop and assorted sex toys. We're taking sex—and, not coincidentally, relationships—to a whole new level through camera phones, SMS text messaging, and mobile phone dating services.

The sex-tech that exists outside the internet owes some of its development and its adoption to the online community. Would we take so quickly to text messaging on cell phones, or to using mobile instant message machines like Sidekicks and Blackberries, if we weren't already accustomed to the idea of real-time text communication?

Cell phones may have become common more than a decade ago, but we're just on the verge of realizing the effects 24/7 connectivity has on our sex lives. The pioneers may well be the adulterers and the teenagers, both of whom have obvious reasons for appreciating the private nature of texting. Text messaging is more discreet than phone calls and saves you from having to write incriminating information on paper or accidentally archiving it in email. When all you need to say is "Ramada Inn @ 9:30," and you can delete the message as soon as you send or receive it, text messaging is your best bet.

For teenagers, text messaging and portable IM is starting to replace the paper note as the epitome of cool—even if you don't have a mobile device, you want one—and what are you going to talk about when you're a teen besides sex? Teens don't have that breadth of experience and vocabulary that adults have (although they may think they do), but certainly they discuss sex with as much or more fervor than grown-ups do. I imagine the usual teen concerns (who's crushing on who, who's going with who, and who's who) dominate the airwaves just as much as they dominated notebook paper.

As one Sex Drive reader says:

> Sex has always been about communication—we all have our story about when sex was nothing but mechanics. It stinks to go home thinking, "wow, I could have cleaned out the garage." Better communication ensures that everybody is actually getting what they want in life.

With all this communication, it's amazing that we still have misunderstandings, conflicts, drama and crises, right? Of course not. Sometimes I wonder if the more we attempt to communicate, the more amazing it is that we understand each other as often as we do.

Communication Is the Root of All Confusion

What's becoming increasingly noticeable in the sexual revolution 2.0 is that our technology has created a whole new layer of concern when it comes to finding a suitable mate. I call this "connectivity compatibility," and you may have already touched upon this issue in your own life—if not with a lover, then with friends or coworkers. Anyone you have to interact with on a regular basis is going to come under this scrutiny at one time or another.

And while most of us agree that communication is a good thing, we're also finding that different people have different preferences—and tolerance levels—for connectivity within their relationships. Not that long ago, it didn't matter if you craved more attention from your partner throughout the day or when you were apart, because you didn't have much choice. Now, it's more a matter of how to reach out than whether to reach out. Yet if one person prefers significantly more frequent interaction than the other, tension can arise in a relationship as one partner feels neglected and the other feels smothered.

Cell phones are so common in Los Angeles that some restaurants have had to post signs warning people that any phones that ring—or worse, get answered—in the establishment will be confiscated by the management. I saw a sign in San Francisco that said "We are a cell-phone friendly restaurant. As long as you take your phone outside, we'll be friendly." (Personally, I think using a phone in a restaurant should go on your permanent record, and you should have to write in Palm's Graffiti language 100 times: "I will not annoy Regina Lynn with my LOUD CELL VOICE in public.")

Mobile phones deserve some of the credit, or the blame, for our connectivity issues. We've grown accustomed to being able to talk to each other no matter where we are. I'll call my sister from the bookstore to ask whether her daughter already has the book I'm about to buy for her, or my roommate from the grocery store to find out whether we need eggs.

But for the sexy stuff, I lean toward text messaging. After all, the produce aisle is hardly the place to call your lover and describe in excruciating detail exactly what you plan to do to him when he gets home—especially if you have to repeat yourself. "WHAT? HELLO? CAN YOU HEAR ME NOW? I SAID I WAS GOING TO LICK YOUR . . . HELLO? . . . LICK, NOT KICK!"

A text message is just sexier. It's secret, and its character limit allows for creative pacing.

E-courtship creates the expectation that you will continue to regale each other with daily (at least!) epistles in email, IM and SMS long after your real-world relationship has solidified. And problems can arise when one party craves the online interaction while the other can't wait to dispense with it and get on with the face-to-face.

To me, a relationship without an online component just sounds dull. I've never been accused of being high-maintenance—just the opposite, I've been told I'm too self-maintained—but I recognize that I have a high desire for internet intimacy. It doesn't have to be sexual (well, not all the time), but it has to be something: an email about his day, a new joke, an IM session before (or from) bed.

I've found that if a man doesn't interest me online, he doesn't interest me offline either. I can't truly get to know a person anymore without email or IM. This doesn't matter so much for professional or social contacts, but in a steady lover, I want that depth. We're different in our writing, funnier, braver, more intimate. I want to know that side of him—and I really notice when it's missing. (I also notice when someone makes the extra effort because he knows it makes me happy. Thanks, you-know-who-you-are.)

I'm not the only one who expects (dare I say, demands) internet interaction with a mate. One Sex Drive reader observed that "relationships nowadays are almost completely online. ... With schedules as hectic as they are, and personal lives not meshing well with professional lives, most talking in a dating relationship, even in real life, is done over IMs throughout the day ... or emails in the evening."

Another reader admitted that she and her husband IM from different rooms in the same house. "Our parents and non-tech friends think we are crazy but if that's the way you've gotten used to getting your info, it works," she said.

While still in the throes of writing this book, I justified my purchase of a handheld computer so I could write anywhere—and have wireless internet access so I could "look stuff up" as needed. Of course, the first thing I did was install Agile Messenger, a free all-in-one IM client for Pocket PC. I had to spend an entire evening chatting from the handheld just to make sure it worked before I could even think about putting my manuscript on the handheld.

For those of us who feel sorry for our ancestors, who had to fall in love and nurture relationships without the internet, connectivity can be A Big Deal. And for anyone who invested a lot of time and thought into email love letters, or who reveled in the nakedness of late-night IM, dropping those elements from the established relationship is the modern update to the cliché, "you don't bring me flowers anymore."

The trick, of course, is to find people who have a similar affection for—or dislike of, I suppose—internet-enabled communication. Couples who meet online have a good chance of assessing their connectivity compatibility. But what if you met in a more traditional place, like a party, a grocery store, or a Sierra Club singles' hike?

You still exchanged email addresses, didn't you?

When I first wrote about "connectivity compatibility" in my column, I apparently touched a nerve. Readers emailed me in ALL CAPS, livid that I would suggest "replacing" face-to-face interaction with IM, or that online relationships were superior to real-world relationships. I'm not sure how they got that idea. I asked several friends to re-read the column with that in mind, to tell me whether I had left out an important word (you'd be surprised how easy it is to drop a "not" when doing any cut-and-paste editing) or if the publishing tool had dropped a paragraph. But nope, no one could see where a reader might get the idea that I promoted online over offline. On the other hand, these are people who know me.

What that column triggered in readers surprised me—and I'm glad they wrote to let me know, even though one man called me deranged, and another speculated that none of my relationships had ever lasted more than six months. Two or three said they thought it was "sick" that the married couple uses IM from different rooms in the same house, as if they no longer communicated by any other means.

All I can say is that if you're not a text-oriented person, that's fine. But if you start dating or even fall in love with someone who is, this really can become an Issue. If you're wondering why your partner is spending a lot more time on the computer, consider what might be going on. It might not be that he or she is seeking a new relationship or a cyber affair—it may just be that you're not the one chatting back, and it hasn't occurred to the blockhead to ask you to. Before you give up, learn the art of seductive text messaging, call your lover at unexpected times, install IM on your handheld and chat for a few minutes during lunch. E-communication might grow on you, but even if it doesn't, it's worth it to give your partner what he or she needs. You might be surprised at how much that can do to rekindle the fires. And if it's not worth it to you? That's important to know, too.

Reach Out and Voice Someone

You knew it had to happen. The vibration setting on your cell phone has finally been harnessed for sex. DialAn Orgasm.com sells a dildo and a butterfly-shaped clitoral stimulator that slip onto your cell phone, translating the vibration setting into something more arousing than a new-call alert. The VibraExciter from VibraFun.com is a small vibrator that can be activated by incoming calls and text messages to any cell phone within range, although it doesn't attach directly to the phone. The device comes with a reminder to be cautious with it in public, as it does not care whose phone is receiving the signal. (But if you don't get a lot of calls, no worries, it works independently too.) I admit that I haven't taken mine out of the house yet. However, extensive testing with several willing volunteers proves the packaging true: the bullet vibrates regardless of whose phone is active.

Yet porn and toys don't even begin to touch the potential of mobile connectivity in the sexual revolution 2.0.

Connecting with each other will always be more popular, *en masse*, than *objects d'amour*.

Phone sex is nothing new. But now technology lets us experiment with gender and species, thanks to voice changers that were formerly the exclusive domain of spies and the paranoid. These devices invite us to explore the dustier sides of our sexual imaginations. It also makes plain-vanilla phone sex more accessible to people who don't think of themselves as adventurous. When the fringe is swapping virtual gender, the mainstream can excuse phone sex with a wave of the hand and an "it's not like it's any big deal, it's just phone sex." And for those in the middle, saying "why don't you be the boy tonight?" is less of a risk over the phone than it is in person, if there's any possibility your partner might double over with laughter at the suggestion.

Voice changers can attach to your phone or come in the form of software with a range of vocal costumes for use with instant messaging, chat rooms and internet telephony.

I talked about phone sex with Midori, a San Francisco sex educator, for one of my Sex Drive columns. Midori is known in certain circles for her workshops such as "Hands-on Flogging" and "Predicament Bondage." But while BDSM is an excellent icebreaker at parties, she finds that one of her most popular classes is "Aural Sex: Seduction by Voice and Erotic Story Telling." I imagine that's because while not everyone wants to admit their fascination with ropes and martinets, almost everyone has a phone.

"I teach people how to use the phone and technology to keep mystery, vibrancy and sexiness in long-term relation-ships as well as in new relationships, without sounding like another stupid come-on," Midori says. The techniques students practice in class "are good for a two-hour or a 20-year relationship." You can use these techniques to seduce a stranger or a spouse, although I wouldn't suggest doing so at the same time unless you're all three into that.

Many of Midori's students take the class to overcome self-consciousness and to learn how to engage in mutual sexual fantasy without feeling silly. To help them gain confidence, she makes a connection between role-playing games and erotic storytelling.

"What needs to happen is to bridge the gap between role playing computer games and the real life role play of people and sex," she says. "It's about regaining that childhood sense of play and mutual permission for the suspension of disbelief, and then combining that with the fundamental libidinous self."

Midori loves the erotic license inherent to voice-changing technology. "If I could morph my body to engage in my fantasies with my lovers, I would, but right now I can't do that yet. I'll settle for my voice," she says, citing a fascination with both Klingon sex and the Japanese film "Ghost in the Shell." ("If I could be her, I would," she says, which is profound, if you've seen the movie.)

In cybersex, the ability to give good word separates the men from the boys. When trolling for real sex, giving good voice is an important and often overlooked skill.

PassionDates.com uses the free Skype telephony client to connect members seeking "discreet intimate encounters," while Match.com's Online SpeedMatching service gives you "four minutes of live phone conversation while you read about and view photographs of your date." While I wouldn't advise launching into erotica in the first four minutes of a Match.com speed date, if you're on camera in the iFriends Adult Community or PalTalk.com, your vocal prowess may be the lure that captures another member's attention.

Whatever the situation, Midori reminds students not to race to the finish line. "Slow it down, make it sweet and sexy, and make sure those pauses count," she says. "A pause lets people stop and think and digest. Combine that with sensory rich description and let the other person fill in that moment of silence with the picture."

She coaches students to inspire interest, build intrigue and set a foundation for future amorous possibilities, and she believes we should all be using our mobile phones to spice up our sex lives.

"We may be dependent on our cell phones these days, but what do we talk about?" she asks. "We say 'hey where are you, how's the party.'" Given our busy schedules and feelings of disconnectedness, she sees an opportunity to bring lovers closer together, talking in real-time or leaving erotic messages throughout the day.

One of her favorite techniques is the erotic cliffhanger, where you figure out the maximum length allowed for a single message on your lover's phone. Call when you know he or she can't answer and start talking. "Go into detail," she says, describing what you'd like to do to them, right now or tomorrow or next week, "and then at exactly the right moment—BEEEEP."

Was It Good 4 U?

Many revolutionaries develop code words and phrases to protect their communications from unauthorized listeners. Secret languages also appeal to our psyches, making us feel as if we belong, as if we're "in" while others are not. Mobile sex is no exception, much to the chagrin of parents of teenagers everywhere.

Most mobile phones offer text-messaging capabilities that let you send messages to other mobile users. Because SMS limits each message to 150, 160 or 224 characters, depending on the service, an entirely new language has developed, much the way chatspeak arose among communities where typing out whole words took too long. Some of the new TXT language is intuitive enough for most native English speakers to figure out. *To* becomes *2*, *for* becomes *4*, *you* becomes *U*. Many of the acronyms stay true to earlier chat media: LOL is still laugh out loud, and A/S/L is still age/sex/location. But it gets more complex from there.

Here's a sample message:

> Hi - Are you going to meet us at the beach? We have the blankets and a bunch of food, but you're going to have to bring your own towel. Oh, I remembered to bring your boogie board, so you're all set. See you there! [214 characters]

And here's the translation from lingo2word.com:

> Hi! RU gunA mEt us @ D bch? w'v D blankets n a bunch of f%d, bt ur gunA hav2 BYO towel. O, I remembered 2 brng ur boogie board, so ur ll set. CU der! [149 characters]

Not all that easy at first sight, is it? Now see what happens when you attempt to get romantic:

> Are you wearing those shoes? Grrrr they're hot. The only thing better than those shoes on your feet is me taking them off your feet. [132 characters]

Here's the translation:

> RU warin doZe shoes? Grrrr they're ht. D
> 11y ting btr thN doZe shoes on ur Ft S me
> takN em off ur Ft. [101 characters]

Not exactly the same feeling, is it? Not to us, anyway. But teenagers are going crazy for SMS lingo and it's likely that as they mature, they won't see much difference between the first passage and the second.

I love text messages. I send them all the time, naughty ones, silly ones, and even important information like "u left ur keys in the door I put them in the flowerpot" when the occasion calls for it. It gives you a different flavor when a lover texts you than when he calls you. A text message isn't as immediate as a phone call and it's more private than talking aloud in a public place. No one is going to want to slap you for texting in a restaurant (as long as your ringer and keypad are set to "silent mode"). I can't say the same for phone calls.

And yet, as positive as I am about sex-tech, I can't see myself ever finding the Lingo sexy. If you do, that's great. And if you're wondering which way you swing, try these on for size (translations follow):

1. I12 lck u frm ur toes 2 ur neck

2. i lov D scent of ur skin, D movement of ur hair, D taste of ur lips

3. DY av NE idea hw mch I lov u? u gro mor btifl evry yr. hpE aNvrsrE

4. ur }xx mak me tremble

5. TY 4 dinA 1st nyt -- n esp 4 D dessert heh heh

Translations:

1. I want to lick you from your toes to your neck.

2. I love the scent of your skin, the movement of your hair, the taste of your lips.

3. Do you have any idea how much I love you? You grow more beautiful every year. Happy anniversary.

4. Your kisses make me tremble.

5. Thank you for dinner last night -- and especially for the dessert, heh heh.

Toothsome? Try Toothing

"Toothing" is one of those things that could only have started on the internet. First, the bloggers at TheTriforce.com decided to play a prank on all of us by "reporting" the practice of initiating—or attempting to initiate—casual sex by flirting with people carrying Bluetooth-enabled mobile devices. Bluetooth is a wireless protocol that allows any Bluetooth-enabled gadget to detect and possibly communicate with any other Bluetooth-enabled gadget within a certain range. Many PDAs and cell phones have Bluetooth, as do Sidekicks and Blackberries.

The concept of toothing is simple. Your device scans the immediate vicinity for other Bluetooth devices. It presents you with a list of those devices' names. You attempt to figure out which of the names on the list correspond to the toothsome babe sitting five rows ahead of you on the subway, or standing farther down the line outside the theater, or sitting on the other side of the coffee house. And then you start to flirt.

All kinds of media jumped on the story, from women's magazines to news media to blogs, from print to broadcast to online. Triforce scrambled to get people in place for the media to interview, people who supposedly had been toothing for sex. They set up a forum where these fake toothers posted where they were going to be toothing at any given time. Conventions, public transportation and clubs seemed to be the most popular locations, for one obvious reason: the more people around you, the more likely you are to find someone to tooth.

It started as a hoax, and for about a year nobody realized it, even though flirting by Bluetooth would be very difficult. It's not like wireless internet, where you can use any number of chat and email clients. As I understand it, you'd have to make initial contact by sending .vcf files, which are basically electronic business cards, back and forth. But the press surrounding toothing may be responsible for selling as many Bluetooth devices as any marketing on the gadget-maker's part. One Sex Drive reader confesses to buying his Treo 650 smartphone after reading an article about toothing, and I occasionally get email from folks asking me for suggestions on where to go to find other toothers.

When Triforce revealed that the whole thing was a joke, the blog stated:

```
    Toothing--beaming a sexual text message
to a random phone on a commuter-packed tube
train--is a bit like going into a crowded
nightclub, throwing a brick at the dancefloor
with a love letter attached, and hoping that
the person it hits will agree to sleep with
you. It's technically possible, and it's not
```

```
going to happen. That made it even better
when the whole world fell for it.
```

And yet the reason the whole world fell for it is that it does seem entirely possible. It's not much different from what many of us have already done. I don't mean throwing bricks in nightclubs. I mean we've hooked up through textual foreplay in chat rooms, over IM, through online dating services, in role-playing games, in email discussion groups, even through the company Lotus Notes system if we're comfortable living on the edge. And toothing, aside from the obstacle of not having an easy way to beam your message, is not much different from approaching a babe in person and flirting with him or her in hopes of sparking reciprocal interest.

The hoax may have backfired. What Triforce started as a protest to the new-at-the-time term "dogging," which is British slang for "having sex in a public place," may actually have created the very thing the bloggers tried to parody. An article in the *New York Times* ("When a Stranger Calls, From Afar or Nearby," March 24, 2005) describes flirting and meeting people through Bluetooth devices and mentions dating services like BEDD.com that take advantage of the free—and anonymous—messaging capabilities these devices provide.

What Triforce may or may not have realized was that services similar to the toothing it "invented" already existed, and had for years. But it didn't have a catchy moniker until after the toothing stories came out. (And on the internet, nothing is truly real until it becomes a buzzword.)

MOSOSO-a-go-go

MoSoSo is an acronym for "mobile social software," and it combines elements of toothing, online dating and social networking. Here's how it works.

You sign up at a MoSoSo site—Dodgeball.com seems to be the big one in the United States at the moment—and create a brief profile of yourself. The profile includes a picture and a few words about your interests and your relationship status (committed, available, neither, etc.). That's all, because the profile has to fit on a cell phone. You then invite other users to be on your "Friends" list, and if they accept, they become your Friends. You can also bypass the invitation process by adding as many as five members to your secret "Crush" list.

Then when you go somewhere, you send a text message to Dodgeball that says where you're going. "The Chalet on Colorado Blvd," for example, or " Brainwash @ SOMA." Everyone on your lists who is within a 10-block radius of your location gets the message and can decide whether to run down and meet you there.

Note the terminology here. You have Friends, who must respond to your invitation in order for the service to connect you. And you have Crushes, who you can add to your list without their knowledge. Does this sound like a non-sexual technology to you?

MoSoSo can help you stay in touch with friends or meet new people, whether you're new to the neighborhood or a native to your city. Yet you'll never convince me that sex is not at the heart of it. If you're already in a relationship, why would you need to know that Soxfan32 is at the corner Starbucks?

Why Connectivity Compatibility Matters

Whether spontaneous connection with strangers or ongoing connection with a loved one, the plethora of opportunities we have to communicate with one another is staggering. Tech can be a wonderful way to bring two people closer together—especially if you thought you already knew everything about your partner. Instant messaging in particular reveals a side of someone you didn't know you didn't know about, particularly the person's sense of humor. The way they respond to your message also offers insight, as you learn more about them based on how they translate your intention, tone, body language.

If your relationship started online, the intellectual interchange is what attracted you to one another in the first place. If you lose that connection after the relationship develops offline, you have not allowed your relationship to blossom on all the levels it could. And if one of you is a natural-born text communicator while the other only suffered through the online talking to get to the real world, well, you might need to have a serious talk about what each of you wants and needs from the other.

One of the main themes of this book is our newfound ability to connect with potential lovers all over the world. Yet the internet also gives us the ability to connect with the lover who lives under our own roof, who shares the bathroom and the bed, who takes out the garbage and pays the bills. Why take for granted that person who says, "have a good day, honey," as one or both of you races out the door to travel separately to your separate offices to spend nine hours in separate pursuits? Why not offer a home bound partner a connection to the outside world, a note that you're thinking about her?

Technology often gets blamed for increasing the distance between us. I don't see it that way, but even if we are drifting apart, it's not the *tech* that's doing it. We have the choice of using technology to build deeper, more meaningful connections with one another. Or we can use tech to find quickie sex. The point is, we have a choice in how connectivity informs our relationships. And I think we have an obligation to take advantage of the opportunity to connect in ways that benefit our relationships with ourselves and others.

So there.

Talking About the Revolution

Come to the forum at www.reginalynn.com and share your thoughts on connectivity compatibility.

What are the deal breakers for you when it comes to connectivity compatibility?

Would you like to receive more e-notes from your partner?

How could (or do?) you use your cell phone as a romantic accessory?

Do you prefer voice or SMS? Which does your partner prefer?

REVOLUTIONARY PROFILE
Annalee Newitz

Dr. Annalee Newitz is one of only a handful of writers exploring the wider social implications of technology on our sex lives. Her weekly column, Techsploitation, *is syndicated through AlterNet.com and appears in the* Silicon Valley Metro. *You can also find her articles in* Wired, Salon *and* Popular Science.

What excites you about the sexual revolution 2.0?

Maybe it's because I learned about sex from science fiction, but I think tech enhances our imagination and our fantasies about sex, and ultimately it underscores how diverse our sexuality is. Tech helps remind us that there's no such thing as "normal," that humans are infinitely diverse sexually. It helps you discover what makes you different, sexually, and it helps you find other people who share your desires, too.

I also like the idea that tech extends the capabilities of a body. We use phones to extend our hearing over miles, movies to see things that aren't immediately there, computers to broaden our circle of friends in a way we couldn't do just hanging out in our physical bodies. Tech lets us go beyond what we're born with.

That's something cybersex can do particularly well, as it gives us the chance to explore fantasies that would be impossible to fulfill in real life.

Exactly. And for people who write and read a lot, the medium of text itself is so hot, having that interactive text and the feel of the keyboard can be very sexy. Some of my earliest sexual experiences were in cyberspace—I had cybersex as a teenager—so it doesn't seem freakish to me. Back when I was starting to experiment, it was computers. Before us, it was telephones. It's always something.

You've said you think machines can be very erotic, and yet when you venture outside San Francisco, people still think that bringing tech into the bedroom "doesn't count"—it's not real sex if you use a vibrator or a computer.

That's one thing that I've been disappointed in. It seems like when people write about high tech and they bring in sex, the message always seems to be conservative. People ask me if it's cheating if they flirt online, and the answer they seem to want is that any kind of flirting or sex online is somehow more appalling, more inherently dirty compared to "plain old regular" meeting someone and having an affair. I'm not sure what motivates this. Fear? It doesn't make sense. We're a tool-using species. That's a fundamental part of being human; you can go back a hundred thousand years and people were using tools. It's natural that we use tools in our sex lives, just like we use them for communication, transportation and so on.

Of course, when the automobile came out, people complained about that too. Cars were the dens of iniquity, devilspawn machines. But cars gave you a place to neck, they got you to lover's lane, they let you travel 40 and 50 miles in a night to go on a date. That's what I think about, the broader picture of how we're using all kinds of tools to change our sex lives. It's like, "Hey! A new piece of tech! Let's have sex with it!" Even when we get a super innocent machine like the phone, we figure out how to have sex with it. Or the camera, one of the first things we did was take pictures of people having sex.

It does seem like sex toys have begun to reach a certain level of acceptance now, though.

It's definitely increasingly acceptable to use sex toys, although there's still this idea that it doesn't count. That was part of the whole Clinton/Lewinsky thing, that it wasn't real sex because it was a cigar—a toy—rather than a penis. Actually, that's what made me like Clinton more; instead of your standard "blow me" it was fun and creative, goofing around, playful. And the scandal forced everyone in the nation to think about alternative ways to have sex.

It also spurred a huge demand for cigar porn, for a while.

You mentioned keyboards. I guess I'm not the only one who likes the feel of certain keyboards under my fingers!

When I was at MIT, I did a study where I interviewed people who were aroused by computers—the actual machines. They talked a lot about how the keyboard itself was erotic, and that some keyboards were sexy and some weren't. It makes sense. Fingers are so sensitive, we use them for all kinds of erotic things. Keyboards were a huge part of what did it for them.

Or the server room—there's nothing hotter than a server room, racks of machines humming around you. I've had sex in a server room.

But aren't server rooms refrigerated to keep the machines from overheating?

The hot person in there with you is the key!

3

Cybersex: It's Not Just for Nerds Anymore

Viggo_23   sliding my hand up your smooth, smooth thigh

Aphrodite   mmmm

Viggo_23   you're warm!

Aphrodite   *presses closer* always hot with you

Viggo_23   resting my palm on your hip, fingers lightly stroking your skin

Aphrodite   flicking my tongue along your collarbone

Aphrodite   finding that hollow … right … there …

Viggo_23   mmmm baby yessssss

Viggo_23   storking your belly

Aphrodite   storking! LOL

Viggo_23   LOL stroking i mean, no storks here

Aphrodite   let's hope not!

Aphrodite   mmm you smell clean and male

Aphrodite   i nibble my way up to your earlobe and arch my back

```
Aphrodite  nipples against your chest
Aphrodite  thighs against your thighs
Viggo_23   i'm so hard … feel it on your
           leg … between your legs
```

Sounds silly, doesn't it? Cybersex—like actual sex, now that I think about it—always looks ridiculous from the outside. Yet good cybersex is so much more than the words on the screen, so much more than the excerpt above. It can be such a profound erotic connection between two people that they forget their surroundings and "see" only the interaction; their bodies respond as if they were really touching, and their emotions don't always know the difference.

Cybersex is not the whole of the sexual revolution 2.0, and in fact I don't even think it's the largest part of it, but it certainly has gotten a lot of press in the past decade. Infidelity, divorce, addiction—you name it, there's an article out there warning us *en masse* about the dangerous cesspit that is the internet. What hasn't been written about quite as much is the positive effects of cybersex for individuals, or what the popularity of cybersex can tell us about modern relationships. Without discounting the devastation a person can wreak on her family and herself through cybersex, I am going to concentrate on the positive in this chapter.

In fact, I probably concentrate on the positives throughout this book, because that is my natural bent and it's honestly how I see the convergence of sex and tech. I am definitely aware of the dark side—how could I not be?—but so much has already been written about the evils of the internet that it seems redundant to give it a lot of page space herein.

Long gone are the days when nerds had cybersex all to themselves. Cybersex has become a household word—and in some cases, a household activity. Geek lore claims that the reason we have broadband is to support porn downloads and webcam sex; the reason we have instant messaging is to have cybersex in real-time instead of waiting for email. Yet the implications of cybersex extend far beyond its ability to inspire technological inventions. This is truly a new frontier of romantic relationships, and we have only begun to see the greater role that cybersex will play on the sexual stage in the years to come.

What, you may be asking, is cybersex? I'm sure you already have an inkling, but to preserve appearances (nudge nudge, wink wink), let me tell you how I see it.

Cybersex, also known as "cyber" or "cybering," is consensual sexual interaction among two or more adults using the internet as the primary means of connection. I generally think of cybersex as a text-based activity because that's my preference and that's the way it has been done for decades, but cyber can also include audio chat, avatar-based communities and webcam conferencing.

I don't count pay-to-play services (where you pay a fee to interact with a performer on the other end of the line) as cybersex. The closest actual world parallel to paid cyber is attending a nudie bar, or watching interactive pornography. You pay, she performs, both parties hopefully come away satisfied. On the other hand, actual sex with a performer, whether porn star or prostitute, does constitute actual sex, so the analogy is not watertight. Whatever—it's not an exact science.

Did I mention that cybersex often, but not always, involves at least one of the participants masturbating?

The M Word

Never before in history has it been possible to get off with so many different people. Cybersex has made sex—or at least shared masturbation—available to anyone, anytime, regardless of location, gender, age, appearance, shyness, disability, marital status or other characteristics that affect how we find sexual partners offline.

Though cybersex bears a social stigma even greater than masturbation itself—apparently masturbating *while at the computer* is worse than plain-vanilla masturbation—it has been a cornerstone of internet life from the beginning. It certainly makes masturbation more fun, or at least adds a complex and fascinating dimension to what is otherwise a fairly simple process.

And because everyone does it, people are learning to become more candid about their cyber habits—at least with other people they meet online. You can hardly pretend to be shy about touching yourself if you are planning to do so in collaboration with another person. In fact, in some parts of California and some online dating sites, self love is *in*. We talk about masturbation and cybersex at dinner parties (well, at least the ones I get invited to), we recommend sex toys to our friends, we even stage an annual *menage a moi* for a good cause. Good Vibrations declared May to be National Masturbation Month, and sponsors the annual Masturbate-a-Thon to raise money for sex education organizations like The Center for Sex and Culture in San Francisco. (In 2004, the event raised almost $4,500 in donations. The site said "It's like a walkathon, raising money through pledges. Only doing this event, your feet won't get tired!")

MasturbateForPeace.com received more than 17,000 petitions from 91 countries in 2004, each one representing an individual's commitment to "masturbate in [his or her] own way, focusing [his or her] thoughts and energy towards love and peace." Why? Because "any real love must start from within. You can't love others without loving yourself first." The site offers several helpful suggestions for getting started, including using lubricants and sex toys.

Yes, California has its own little bubble of sexual mores, but it only takes one Google search to prove that we aren't the only state in the union or the world with a healthy interest in autoeroticism. Cybersex has helped many people, particularly women, to become comfortable with masturbation. It's like ice hockey. At first, the skating part seems difficult. Then someone hands you a stick and points you toward the puck and you forget all about learning to skate, you just do it naturally as an extension of the real activity: hockey. Cyber is the same way. You might not feel relaxed and comfortable alone in your bed with a bottle of Astroglide, but when you make masturbation part of an online relationship, it comes naturally. No pun.

It's generally accepted among sex educators that people who masturbate have better sex lives, in part because learning about your body yourself helps you communicate to your partner what you want him or her to do. For people who have to overcome shame or embarrassment in order to touch themselves, the process of learning to masturbate often leads to a greater confidence with partner sex as well. After all, how can you expect a partner to know what gives you pleasure if you don't know it yourself? And if you don't want to touch yourself "down there," why would you expect someone else to want to?

Yet if cybersex were just masturbation, it would hardly be powerful enough to lure people to leave their spouses, to move across the country, or to give up sleep and work in order to spend more time in cyberspace.

Where Is the Good Stuff?

I came into cybersex in the mid-1990s, when I still had to jump through a couple of hoops to join the adult community I'd found on a fledgling website. One of the regulars told me about internet relay chat (IRC) and how I could use it to access the chat room without going through the clunky web interface. (The web interface required you to enter your text into a field, then wait. The page refreshed every 20 seconds or so and listed all the text the participants had typed during the previous 20 seconds. Believe it or not, this was exciting at the time, especially because we could choose different font colors. Oooooo.)

I installed mIRC (an IRC client for Windows) and learned enough commands to get to the room using IRC. Soon after that, the site administrators created a Java-based interface for the website that did about the same thing Java-based chat rooms do now, but by then I was geeking out with IRC and I scoffed at Java like all true chatters.

But then AOL made IRC accessible to the masses. Suddenly, you didn't have to be a techie to cyber. Cybering had only recently become a public phenomenon, with the media jumping on the infidelity and addiction angle and author Deb Levine coming out with the first (and possibly only) "how-to" book about cybersex, *The Joy of Cybersex*. Therapists began to pay attention as marriages suffered and dissolved because of a partner's emotional investment in, or obsession with, cybering.

It was "pretty much the universal death knell of some of the big hangouts, as if a half-thousand Paris Hiltons suddenly showed up to the best party ever," wrote Garrett, a Sex Drive reader. Still, he says, "nerds being nerds, there's always a solid group that knows enough about the technology to stay just outside the mainstream."

Our community managed to withstand an onslaught of newbies trolling for cyber, insistent and rude and ignorant or dismissive of the netiquette. We absorbed the intelligent and strengthened our defenses to weed out the obnoxious.

Our room was like any other of the time. A mix of married, single, divorced; ages ranged from 20 to 60 and beyond. The regulars were smart people who liked to read and write—because if you don't like to read and write, you're unlikely to be drawn to chat. Almost as many women appeared as men, talking as much about non-sexual matters as about sex. In fact, after the initial burst of excitement at finding cybersex, most of the participants came back for the conversation more than the masturbation. Cyber still happened, especially as people paired off and developed one-on-one relationships through instant messaging, but the main room was a place where we could relax after (or sometimes, during) a hard day at work and talk about anything. And I do mean anything.

For whatever reason, our room had several nurses. I'm rarely sick but when I do get something, I get it bad. I'd been coughing and miserable for almost two weeks, and starting to get worried because every breath was an agony, so I started breathing as shallowly as possible. This doesn't lend itself to the deep thought my job required. I brought it up in the room, and the Nursing Brigade had a public confab and diagnosed me with pleurisy. Pleurisy is an inflammation of the membrane that lines your lungs, and its symptoms are painful breathing and misery. It is not in the least bit sexy. But the banter flowed as I described my symptoms, pretending to be on my death-bed and leaving my (imaginary) possessions to my chat buddies. The nurses took advantage of the sexy-nurse cliché while discussing possible illnesses. I can't remember now if my doctor concurred with the diagnosis, but the room did force me to go to the doctor and take antibiotics and get better.

These days, if you want to find your own adult community, with or without a Nursing Brigade, you have to dig deeper.

"At some time I cannot pinpoint," says Wendy, a member of the Sex Drive forum, "a set of people started using chat as a way to make the contact to meet or call others for sex, like it was one big pool of people waiting for an offer. . . . Whatever happened to chatting to converse? It's getting more and more difficult to find someone who'll type more than three words a line and actually spell out words." Perhaps the popularity of online dating sites changed how the masses felt about chat. Or maybe the 14-year-olds and the spam bots just became too prevalent for grown-ups to want to deal with, so the real chatters had to find safer places to meet.

And while I'm on the subject, logging into a chat room and typing "any hrny ladez want 2 make me cum?" does not lead to good cyber. It's also not going to lead to offline sex, so why anyone wastes his time with such nonsense is beyond me.

Good cybersex requires imagination, communication, emotion. It always involves an element of suspense, because you can't be certain what the other person will do. In fact, great cyber has something in common with great sex: a relationship. Whether that's a one-hour stand or a 10-year engagement, it's the relationship that elevates cybersex from the silly to the sublime.

And that's why good cybersex has gone underground. Not long ago, just being online meant you had something in common with the people you chatted with. Today, with 68 percent of American households connected to the internet—and more than half those enjoying the thrill of high-speed connections—it's almost impossible to find someone with compatible desires, skills and schedules on a random swoop through chat.

Good cyber is thriving, beyond the reach of the newbies, the opportunists, the clueless and the bots. It happens on premium sites like PalTalk, which one friend of mine describes as "an international circle jerk," although the service is not all, or even primarily, about the adult communities. It arises out of environments like forums and email discussion groups, when members click and begin to talk to each other in private. I know of at least one pair of Sex Drive forum members who enjoyed a cybersex affair and continued to stay in touch as email friends. Cybersex also blossoms in gaming communities, ranging from online canasta to complex massive multiplayer online role-playing games (MMPORGs). It seems that having a common interest and something else to do can lead, expectedly or unexpectedly, to hot online sex just as it can lead to hot offline sex. Who woulda thunk it?

Cybersex is also an element of online dating. That was one of the findings that surprised Dr. Janet Lever, sociology professor at California State University, Los Angeles, when she conducted the *Cybersex and Romance Survey* for ELLE magazine in 2004. "A lot of people using the dating sites never really wanted to meet anyone," she said. "It turns out that almost an equal number of people met someone through chat rooms. The chatters ended up dating and sometimes getting married, and the people using online personals often were just involved in chat and flirtation and not really meeting."

Good cybersex may emerge where an outsider least expects it, but that doesn't mean it's rare. Of the 15,000 respondents to the ELLE survey, 53 percent of women and

81 percent of men reported participation in adult chat rooms, sex newsgroups or live webcam sex.

Teledildonics

The technologies that facilitate cybersex encounters have expanded far beyond the text-based BBSes (electronic bulletin boards) of the last century, although ancient peoples found those as stimulating as webcams are to us. Services like There.com offer sophisticated graphics that let you build avatars—animated characters—to represent you in the chat rooms. Among PalTalk's communities are many video chat rooms where men and women with webcams log in to flirt, talk and cyber. Even plain-vanilla IM has caught on; Yahoo Messenger and MSN Messenger both allow users to publish and view webcams, while Apple's proprietary iChatAV client and iSight webcam seem designed, if not marketed, for cybersex.

And then you have teledildonics, the first real step toward actualizing virtual sex. Even sophisticated sex toys like the CybOrgasMatrix robotic sex doll and the hardware-heavy Virtual Sex Machine focus more on masturbation than sexual relationships. Teledildonics takes the best of sex toys, adds a sophisticated layer of communication, and helps people come together regardless of how many miles lie between them.

Online community pioneer Howard Rheingold is credited with coining the term "teledildonics" in his 1991 book *Virtual Reality*. It may not be a household word yet, but recent developments in this field have finally begun to realize its potential, and I'm betting it won't be long before "teledildonics" hogs the headlines as much as "cybersex" does now.

Sinulate Entertainment owns several patents on "remote interaction technology." I had a nice long chat with CEO Steve Rhodes, who extolled the virtues of the Sinulator, pointed out its role in helping soldiers stationed in Iraq make love to their wives back home, and sent me the product for my review, not necessarily in that order.

The Sinulator is a device that lets you connect a sex toy to your computer so other people can control it for you over the internet. Mine arrived the morning of the day I was giving a party. I signed, sent the UPS guy on his way, and returned to my preparations without even opening the box. It wasn't until hours later, with about 20 friends draped around the room, that I remembered my new toy.

After announcing to the room that I had one of these, I really had no choice but to open the box and pass the thing around. If you've ever been to a baby shower, you're familiar with the "oooohs" and "aaaaahs" that ensued. We were all impressed with the surprisingly substantial Rabbit Pearl vibrator, which features rotating plastic pearls in the shaft and a vibrating bunny for external stimulation. Also, it's pink.

Here's how it works. Your Sinulator package includes a transmitter, a vibrator and a receiver. When it's installed and the client is running, you attach your toy to the wireless receiver and switch it on. Finally, you go to sinulator.com and choose a name for your toy. After that, anyone who knows your toy's name can set your toy a-buzzin' using the Sinulator control panel available at the website. Neither of you have to register or divulge any personal information—not even an email address.

The control panel looks like a grown-up version of a driving toy for baby, with buttons and levers and sliders that you manipulate with your mouse. I laughed when I first saw it—now you can have sex and drive a racecar at the same time! You don't have to download anything, and you can run it from almost any browser, even the one on your handheld computer or PDA.

But that's not all.

Sinulate.com has also created the Interactive Fleshlight. With this gadget, a man doesn't need a mouse to control his lover's vibrator. The Fleshlight is a standard sleeve-style vibrator for men, with a twist: it's also a transmitter. You attach it to your computer and slide your penis into it and start moving. The device measures the speed and force of each thrust and communicates those metrics to the software, which translates them into vibration and pulse on the other end.

In other words, a man can be thrusting in Cleveland while a woman is penetrated in Seattle, and the cybersex experience gets one step closer to the Star Trek holodeck.

Like classic cybersex, and in fact like actual sex, good Sinulator sex relies on communication. The better your communication, the better your Sinulator experience will be. As with real sex, you can thrust too hard or too fast, or finish too soon, or not finish at all. Just watching my vibrator propel itself across my desk onto the floor was enough to tell me that anyone who wants to spend time with me is going to have to use the Jackhammer button sparingly, or it's going to be over real quick. (You can set local overrides, so no matter what the other guy does, the vibrator won't exceed the intensity levels you set. But we don't have to tell him that, now, do we?) You can leave each other hanging or draw the experience out as long as you can stand it. If you're on your own, you can log on to the Sinulator webcam network, pick a performer and pay to play.

Remote interaction technology has true potential to bring people together. If you travel often, or if you're in a long distance relationship, this technology provides another avenue for intimacy, especially if it's hard for you to use toys with a partner when you're in the same room. The Sinulator can help couples become more comfortable with sexual adventure—something 40 percent of the "Primetime Live" American Sex Lives 2004 survey respondents wished for.

The Sinulator is not the only entry in the teledildonics field, although they own the patent on the technology. HighJoy.com seems to be the first site to combine explicit online personals with teledildonics. This company is gambling that people who start with cybersex often want to proceed to real sex. At press time, HighJoy.com had "soft-launched," meaning that a website is up and running even though the full service isn't. I'm watching it closely.

And yet even with something as sophisticated as the Sinulator, it's not the technology. It's what you do with it that counts.

It's in the Brain

Technology is only a facilitator. It is not the heart of cybersex. And no matter how many vibrators you connect to how many browser-based control panels, such devices will not replace the most important element of good cyber, which, not coincidentally, is also a necessary ingredient in good actual sex: imagination. If you are older than about 23, the true eroticism of cybersex happens in the mind. Even with the emergence of teledildonics, where one person's actions control the physical stimulation for the other, it would be a poor substitute for the real thing if you didn't engage your imagination.

No one believes cybersex is going to replace actual sex. But many have welcomed it into their lives as an adjunct to in-person sex, or even a temporary substitute for the real thing. It's not just a sexual outlet that brings no risk of disease or pregnancy. It also has to do with intimacy.

Yes, that's right, I said intimacy.

Online relationships develop differently than offline relationships, progressing from the inside out. When you meet someone in an adult community online, whether it's text-only, avatar-based or webcam chat, you have both already indicated you are interested in sexual interaction. Otherwise, why log on to that particular community? Even if you're not in the mood for mutual masturbation, your very presence in the community says you are open to and looking for some sort of stimulation, be it witty banter, dirty talk or falling in love. You don't have to stumble through a first date, you don't have to wine and dine, you don't have to establish your physical appearance or income or employment or any other personal characteristic before you can chat up a potential partner. All you have to do is show up and start talking. And if you give good word, you just might get somewhere.

One caution, though. I noticed after a few weeks of chatting in an adult room that my "appropriateness filters" changed. Ribald jokes and sexual subject matter no longer seemed out of the ordinary, and I would catch myself in the middle of a story in situations other than the chat room, realizing too late that what I was saying was not suitable for the occasion. It was a good thing I was freelancing full time and didn't unleash any of my new-found potty mouth in an office!

I have talked to dozens of people who have found cyber to be the best thing they ever did for their offline sex lives. In his book *Love Online: Emotions on the Internet*, professor Aaron Ben-Ze'ev finds a recurring theme: women who report experiencing their first orgasms through cybering. Some say their online sex was the best sex of their lives, and many of those go on to bring their new-found understanding into face-to-face relationships. One man I know who had avoided sex for 14 years, having suffered repeated sexual abuse and rapes as a child, finally overcame his fear of intimacy by practicing in cyberspace.

Cybersex can be a onetime thing, with a new partner each time. It can even shift constantly to new venues such as chat rooms you've never visited. Yet most people seem to gravitate toward a particular community or a particular lover, once they find people with whom they feel at ease. No matter how many adult communities are available to us at any given time, it's a challenge to find a place where you want to spend a lot of time. Which means that when you do, you return often, become a "reg" (regular), and forge friendships and cybersex relationships with the other regs.

It's in those relationships where we find the peculiar intimacy that is cyber. That's where we start with our innermost feelings and work outward. For many of us, that's a completely new experience—it would be like mailing someone your diary before a first date. It can set us up for the most painful heartbreaks, particularly because it's not yet acceptable in our society to cry on someone's shoulder over a cyber breakup, and yet every person who experiences that type of emotional connection online brings that realization to his or her offline relationships.

And anyone who doubts that an online relationship is a real relationship has not been paying attention.

Cybersex is so immersive that when you compare an actual sexual relationship to your cyber love life, it's often the real world that seems lacking, at least for a while. One

Sex Drive reader relates an experience many of us have had with cyber:

> What's interesting is that you one day wake up and take a look around and notice "damn, this is not the way I want to live my life." So I uninstalled mIRC and everything is straightened out (but it took a while I might add). Since online chatting tends to be very intense, almost like a rush, it's easy to get hooked.

When people talk about internet addiction, they usually mean cybersex and porn, which often go hand-in-hand anyway (er, no pun intended). At press time, a Google search on "cybersex" resulted in sites dealing with cyber-sex addiction, healing marriages after cyber affairs, and pedophilia. I expected links to several chat rooms and porn sites, but they are outnumbered by the recovery sites.

Cybersex is indeed a powerful siren, one that sings to men and women alike. In an article published by internet protection software developer ContentWatch, author Mark B. Kastleman writes:

> [Cybersex] takes decent, intelligent, respected and successful women and **makes them stupid!** Just as it does for men, … cybersex becomes a "drug of choice" where women find pleasure, relief and escape (self-medication) from the pain, stress and realities of everyday life. (his emphasis)

I can't fully discuss cybersex without noting just how powerful a force it is. Cybersex addiction sets in more easily than most people think. Even now I would be skeptical about the sheer number of articles addressing addiction and recovery if I hadn't come close to being One of Those People myself.

I was never addicted to cybersex in the true sense of the word, and no, that's not denial. Over time, addicts give up other activities to engage in their addiction, and stories abound of people avoiding family gatherings and professional events in order to have more time to cyber. In my case, I actually became more social offline than I had been before I started chatting, and I continued to be a workaholic, putting in long hours in my freelance business. I exercised regularly and ate well, read novels and went to the movies, just as I had always done (and still do, for that matter).

Most importantly, I finally discovered a sexual enthusiasm of my own, and I blossomed into a truly sexual being for the first time in my life. I was 26.

The intimacy that evolves online—that makes online friendships so powerful and discussion groups so companionable—can become more alluring than one's actual relationships. Some people have thrown away their marriages and families in an attempt to bring that intimacy to life outside the internet, not realizing that online intimacy is a different kind of connection than day-to-day intimacy. I'm not saying it's fake or unimportant, only that it is particular to the medium.

That's the sad side of cybersex. We often develop technology faster than we can figure out how to use it in a mature or positive manner. The casualties of cybersex gone wrong have been the husbands, wives and children of the pioneers. The technology makes emotional infidelity easier, and the intimacy of internet relationships has been so unexpected for many that obsession, if not addiction, sets in almost before we're aware of it.

Yet now, 10 years after cybersex began to hit the front page of the newspaper, we are all aware of the potential to fall prey to its more dangerous appeals. If you're married or committed to a long-term relationship, snap out of the denial—it can happen to you. Or, if you know for sure you could never fall in love online, recognize that other people might fall in love with you.

We can learn to reap the benefits of cybersex without succumbing to the risks, if we pay attention.

(Cyber)Sex Ed

In college, my writing mentor was the professor who taught Children's Literature every spring. Even though the class occupied one of the largest rooms on campus, it always had a waiting list, and I've always regretted I didn't at least sit in, even if I didn't manage to enroll. Apparently the administration felt that children's lit was not academic enough, not a "real" class, and had no intention of allowing Dr. Boe to add other sessions or teach it in the fall as well. But how many of us were going to go on to become scholars of Henry James or even Shakespeare? And how many of us were going to become parents, aunts, uncles, grandparents—roles that practically guarantee we'll be reading to children? Exactly. Why it was more important to study the works of dead men than it was to study the best of children's literature still puzzles me. And I was an English major!

It's the same with sex. We learn so many important life skills as we grow up, from television and movies and advertising as well as from our parents and teachers. How to balance a checkbook, how to make a fashion statement, how to plunge a toilet, how to treat acne, how to get a job, how to jump-start a car battery. Yet how do we get our first practical education about sex? Fumbling with another teenager who doesn't know any more than we do. While there's a certain sweet innocence to those early experiences, even in our modern world, I've always thought we'd have fewer sexual problems as adults if we had a more formal method of induction into the sexual universe.

A ritual akin to the initiation ceremony in Jean Auel's *The Valley of Horses* would suit me fine. Rather than leaving me to my own devices at 17, wouldn't it have been great to look forward to a skilled, attractive adept on my 18th birthday, teaching me communication and technique and pleasure? Perhaps a few weeks of meetings beforehand in which we discussed emotional health, safe sex, birth control and so on? I'm not talking about a boring, scrubbed-clean health class, but a real introduction to the adult sexual universe.

With cybersex, we can combine learning what we like sexually with learning to communicate, to ask for what we want, and to set boundaries about what we don't. We have to listen to each other, to follow one another's cues, if we are to find real fulfillment through virtual sex. Body image worries fall by the wayside; even with a webcam, you can control how much of you the other person sees, and how much remains a fantasy. You don't even have to brush your teeth, although you'd probably get more into it if you did. I used to cyber in sweatpants and wool socks, and to tell my partners exactly what I was wearing, and it never seemed to cool anyone's ardor. If anything, it made the encounter more vivid, more unusual—more real.

Until your first uninhibited cybersex session, you may find it difficult to believe that anyone would engage in such a ridiculous practice. From the outside, it looks a lot like typing, or maybe typing and masturbating. But it can teach us to be better lovers, it can help us recognize the signs of our own arousal and fulfillment, it can make each one of us the star in our own erotic story. Cyber allows us to explore fantasies and engage both body and imagination in sexual pleasure. (And boy howdy does sex get hot when you do that!)

Cybersex raises our expectations and helps us explore—and reach past—our boundaries. If we can bring this newfound self-knowledge into actual relationships, bring the intimacy of the mind-to-mind connection that cyber shows is possible, imagine just how deep an offline relationship can go if we are willing to be as open with a lover face-to-face.

For all the advances in cybersex technology that most basic element of all still remains: shared storytelling. The real appeal of cybersex is and will always be connecting with another person. That's one reason women take to cybersex so naturally, even if porn does nothing for them.

Why Women Love Cybersex

Women who cyber, love it. In cyber, we are guaranteed something we might not find if we were to seek out a sexual encounter in real life: focused, admiring sexual attention. A person who doesn't feel like interacting simply doesn't log on. Thus, if a woman ventures into an adult community, she can do so with confidence that someone will to want to talk.

Or better yet, write. I'm not saying that audio and video don't have a place in cybersex. But women love to be wooed with the written word. If Cyrano had realized just how powerful his prose would be, he never would have bothered with that silly boy, Christian. There's something so intimate about writing and reading that combining sex with chat can have unexpectedly serious consequences, not the least of which is carpal-tunnel syndrome. (Yeah, right, you developed that at work.)

In *Love Online*, Aaron Ben-Ze'ev observes: "In cyber-space, that which often remains unspoken must be put into words." The wordplay and sensual imagery of great cybersex attracts us because it requires both parties to be present and to communicate. It's like starring in your own erotic story. Even when you add the visual excitement of a webcam, you can't tune out and turn a woman on in cybersex. Which means cyber is good training for anyone who wants to upgrade their sex lives. And it's not only a way to spice up a relationship, it can teach you things about your partner's desires that one or both of you might never have suspected otherwise.

Here's how it went for me.

When you're entering a chat room, the first thing you have to do is choose a name for your online self. As a recovering English major I couldn't possibly pick something like "HotChick" or "justlooking"—I needed a name with pizzazz, an intelligent name, a name I would be comfortable in and not forget in case I wanted to come back on another day. "Venus" rhymed with "penis," but "aphrodite" had the right feel to it. It didn't take long for people to abbreviate it as "aph" and I sometimes even logged in as "aph" when I felt like chatting but not cyber-ing. I am probably the only adult chat room regular who kept a dictionary of classical mythology and an English/ Latin dictionary next to the computer at all times.

I also came up with one personal rule: tell no lies in the room. I was not going to pretend to be wearing a thong and corset if I wasn't, and I was not going to say I was heading out for a job when really I was headed to the kitchen for ice cream. I didn't lie about my age, bra size, hair color or jeans preference either.

But given the chance, I would make a joke.

That was the best part of chat. I could give my sense of humor—especially the naughty bits—free rein. Many of the other regulars were intelligent and quick-witted as well, and our verbal volleys dominated the room.

Not to say that people didn't double- and triple-up into steamy sessions in both public and private windows. But the banter often took precedence over the sex, and often people logged on just to see what was going on in people's lives. If you've been there, you know what I'm talking about. If you haven't, it might be hard for you to believe the strength of community bonding if the mix is right. I think I was exceedingly lucky to hit upon that room when I did, with that bunch of people, for it is much harder today to wander into a free adult chat room now and find the same level of intelligence and community. If you want to find that kind of interaction, you may to have to join a premium service.

What I learned from that experience goes far beyond the momentary titillation of "computer sex." Before cybersex, I could not learn to enjoy oral sex, either giving or receiving. Early childhood trauma had programmed my body memory to treat oral sex as an assault, not a pleasure, and I would shut down despite my best efforts to remain engaged.

After writing about oral sex—among many other activities I had yet to feel comfortable about during actual sex—I found that I began to lose the fear, and in fact to develop an interest in the real thing. Having expended so much energy in finding new ways to describe old actions, and seeing how turned on my partners were when I went there, I found that I could resist my body's urge to disappear. My newfound enthusiasm soon spread to a much wider range of sexual pleasure than I had experienced before, and to this day I know I owe much of my current state of sexual satisfaction to my time as aphrodite.

Lest you think I'm a special case, I should tell you that *Love Online: Emotions on the Internet* is full of such stories, and that I personally know several other people for whom cybersex was a healing experience. In fact, when I have written columns about the dark side of cybersex, I then receive letters from counselors who tell me that their clients have found it to be a positive experience in their lives. But it's not going to work for everybody, so *caveat emptor*. Or *caveat chatter*, as the case may be.

Women respond to cybersex because we respond to words, to emotion, to cleverness and imagination. We like the fantasy, the fact that it must be mutual, that both part- ners must be present to win. I know it's a cliché, but what we find in cybersex is what many of us want in actual life even if we don't know how to ask for it: pre-, during- and post-coital conversation. Cyber is a place for us to practice talking dirty, using language and issuing commands that at first do not come naturally to delicately raised ladies. It is a place where we are encouraged to let our hair down and dance on the tables, to add some shimmy to the shake, to leave our decorum at the door.

It is a place where a woman can put on her little French maid outfit and play submissive, or don the leather mask and whip some man into shape. The fan- tasies that nice girls somehow learn to suppress and fear (while their brothers are sneaking peeks at pornography and dreaming about Lara Croft) can not only come out and play, they can achieve more dimensions because we can experience them with other people—in a safe, com- fortable environment.

What a woman explores online may not be what she's comfortable with offline. But when she meets her lovers in person, she appreciates their insight into her sexual fantasies, even if she doesn't act out everything she's ever discussed. That doesn't mean the mystery is gone. Every one of us has our own sexual yays and nays; cybersex helps us figure out the rules and communicate them to one another before the actual meeting.

A person who can woo a others in an online community often develops greater confidence in approaching and talking with prospects in the actual world. Obviously you shouldn't be as explicit or probably move as fast in person as you can in the free-for-all of the internet, but words and imagination are words and imagination wherever you are. Use them!

Why Cybersex Matters

Cybersex matters, all right. Imagine the ripple effect of thousands upon thousands of people exploring their sexuality in the privacy of their own homes but with the feedback of others. Dr. Lever's survey found that 28 percent of women and 37 percent of men felt that sex on the internet had "expanded the boundaries of what they found erotic." A whopping 60 percent of women and 44 percent of men who ventured into new sexual territory online later mentioned their desires to their real-life partners.

Whether this led to exciting new sex or slaps across the face doesn't matter. The important thing is that we have a way to probe our deepest desires, to discover responses and fantasies we didn't know or admit we had, to try out in our imaginations things we aren't ready to bring into our actual sex lives. And when that many people become that much more in tune with their sexual capacities, it can't help but infuse and shape their future relationships.

Cybersex teaches us to communicate about sex. Chat forces us to put our wants and actions into words; webcams present a particular challenge for body language, as you try to fit yourself into that little frame without looking ridiculous on the other end. Audio chat requires you to say those naughty things *out loud*, where other people can hear you.

Asking for what we want, and being asked for what someone else wants, is a skill many of us could stand to improve. I know I am much more articulate about what I want to give and receive—verbally and non-verbally—because of the practice two years of cyber gave me. Text was and still is my favorite, but I've done my share of audio and video sex too. If you engage in cybersex and don't learn something about communication, you should probably go back to surfing porn.

If you've never cybered, it's hard to understand the siren call of the online relationship. It looks silly from the outside, even if you accept intellectually that it's not about the computer, it's about the people. Yet for some, immersion in cybersex has resulted in poor job performance, in addiction, in divorce, and not just for folks who were bound for Jerry Springer one way or another. It's not like television; it doesn't have an Off switch. Many intelligent people—men as well as women—learn that despite their best intentions, they cannot compartmentalize themselves so thoroughly as to leave cyber in cyberspace. Why?

Why is cybersex so compelling that people sacrifice so much to it? What does cybersex provide that offline relationships don't? And can we—should we—bring whatever that is into our offline relationships?

When we can answer these questions, we'll be on our way into a new level of relating. Because right now we're still figuring out, one individual at a time, what cybersex feeds us that nothing else does. If we pay attention, we start to see—and, even more difficult, to admit—what we hunger for in our offline lives. Is it attention? Is it love? Creativity? Novelty? Maybe it is something as simple as appreciation, being viewed as a sexual being after mortgages and kids and yard work and gravity wreak havoc on our bodies, our schedules and our energy levels.

Talking About the Revolution

Come to the forum at www.reginalynn.com and share your thoughts on cybersex.

Did cybersex seem shocking when you first heard about it? How do you feel about it now?

Have you pushed your sexual boundaries with cybersex?

Would you consider using teledildonics with your real-life lover? Why or why not?

REVOLUTIONARY PROFILE
Pat & Steve

*Pat and Steve are the co-founders of Sinulate Entertainment, the com-
pany that made internet-controlled sex toys a reality. I spoke with them
at length because they are doing the more to harness technology's
potential to transform relationships than any other company today.*

**You've told me that you have customers who say the Sinulator
saved their marriage. How?**

Here's one example. We have a customer whose husband is
an executive at a publicly traded company. They live in Nantucket,
where she is an at-home mom, but he works in Los Angeles.
She says sex has always been a part of their lives, a big part of
their communication. They started off with phone sex, which is
fine, but there are only so many things you can say to turn
somebody on. She found our product, and she bought it, and
now she says they have used it every weekday for eight or nine
months. He will physically be in his office in Los Angeles and
control the toy for her. Now they've taken the next step and
she's controlling toys on him, when he's in the Los Angeles
apartment.

We have military couples where one partner is in Iraq. They
get a public computer terminal so the discreet nature of the
system becomes very important. They can't afford the luxury of
downloading an application, but they can launch a browser and
control the toy on their partner back home.

Sex is all about fulfilling some sort of fantasy. The fact that
a person can physically affect the way the other feels is very
important facet of the overall relationship.

**What if the person who is traveling is the one who wants to
use the toy?**

We travel with these things all the time. You can pack it in
your luggage easily, although you might not want to keep the

toys in your briefcase. Pat has never been pulled aside at the airport, although Steve went through security with 10 of them. They opened up his bag and pulled out all the toys.

These people, the airport personnel, they see everything. It's a non-issue, as long as it's not a bomb.

Is the Sinulator cybersex?

I don't know what the real definition of cybersex is. If the definition of cybersex is "I'm having sex with you remotely," then yes. The Sinulator defines reaching out and touching somebody. It's without a doubt the most advanced example of remote sexual interaction.

How so?

For one thing, it's wireless. Our customers have told us they don't want to be plugged in to the computer. With wireless you can roam around: bedroom, bathroom, living room. Anywhere in the house as long as you're in range of the computer. Most women want to be in the bedroom. If you're on webcam you're most likely in the same room as the computer!

We also have two-way transceiver technology. I can have a toy and you can have a toy, and neither of us has to be at the computer to control each other's toys. I can use the handheld controller to control your toy—I don't have to get up and go back to the computer to do that. I can stay on my bed with my toy that's running, put it in the right mode, and send signals to yours. All you need is to be in range of a computer that is on the internet.

Our current product has three times the range of the first one. It works on a global frequency, and we sell it all around the world. It works across all browsers and platforms, and it's fast—in less than half a second, the signal I send from California can move a toy in Eastern Europe.

And the price has come down, from about $200 to about
$100 for a very high caliber product.

What are you working on for the future?

Many people are looking for the full solution: a platform
they can go to where they can control toys, see each other, talk
to each other. We believe that's an important facet of the overall
experience. We're working on that in partnership with companies
that do chat clients, audio/video solutions, that sort of thing.

We want to be enablers. We want the market to grow, not
to keep everything to ourselves. We license the platform to
matchmaking sites, other sites that want to use it. Right now
that includes Camz.com, Bondage.com and LoveVoodoo.com.

Our whole mantra is for people to tell us what they want.
Everybody has their own sexual fantasies, and we want to be
able to fulfill them. Our hope is that the Sinulator will bring
people closer together over time, and allow people to fulfill
fantasies and relationships they would never be able to fulfill
otherwise.

4

Positively Pornographic

challenge you to find any web user who has not gone looking for a naughty picture, however they might define such a thing. Well, obviously, your *mom* hasn't—mine certainly has not—but almost everyone else has.

Few dispute the role of porn in our push for technological innovation. But not everyone realizes how porn influences sex—real sex—in the internet age.

Thanks to the web, men and women have equal access to sexual content in quantities unimagined by previous generations. I'm not going to argue the morality of porn or where I draw the line between entertainment and obscenity, although you'll probably wind up with an idea of where I stand on these issues. Rather, I want to show how this accessibility is changing the way we think about erotic content, where it fits in our relationships, and why its existence is important far beyond sex.

Porn for—and by—the People

Krisen-without-a-T, a 20-something actress and writer, told me once that she figured if her theater career didn't work out, she could always become a stripper because "no matter what you got, someone is willing to pay to see it."

It's true. Whatever turns you on, you will find it online. In that respect, online porn is a lot like online dating: the vastness of the internet proves the old adage "there's someone [or something] for everyone." Not only is there something out there, now you can actually find it. In fact, if you spend enough time online, you will no longer be surprised at anything the human sexual imagination can dream up.

Fetishists and people with alternative sexual desires, or desires they always *thought* were crazy, fringe or otherwise unique to them, have found unprecedented community online. Looners—people turned on by balloons—have not only found each other at balloon porn sites, they have brought this formerly obscure fetish into the public eye (well, the porn-savvy public eye, anyway). Furries, those folks who like to pretend they are foxes or horses or other animals (real or mythological) while sharing their sexual fantasies, have found kindred spirits on the internet.

Online porn can help each of us discover that we're not freaks or deviants, and that others share our particular desires. Thanks to the internet, more of us realize just how normal we are. Or, rather, that Alfred Kinsey was right: when it comes to human sexuality, there is no such thing as "normal."

For more people than you might think, becoming more comfortable with ourselves and with pornography leads to the desire to share that comfort with others. As digital video equipment drops in price, professional producers have been able to create high-quality visuals despite pathetic budgets. And amateurs can create professional-looking movies, whether for their private use or for homegrown distribution. In fact, do-it-yourself is so popular, the Adult Video News annual awards show had to add categories for amateur porn.

The advantages the internet provides to entrepreneurs apply to adult websites as much as to any other business. Services like MyAdultSite.com break down the technological barriers to creating a homemade adult website by providing templates, hosting and support for individuals who want to run their own adult sites without having to learn a lot of the technology.

In 2004, the percentage of households with broadband internet access finally surpassed the percentage of households stuck on dialup. Why? Porn. Oh, they'll tell you it's for digital music and movie downloads, or even for telecommuting. But compare the number of people in your social circle who telecommute to the number of people who sneak peeks at online porn. Uh huh. It's hard to find exact statistics on Americans' porn-viewing habits, as most of the big research firms don't track it. Yet we do know that a lot more women are watching it—and making it—since the internet eliminated the need to drive to Joe's Smut Shack. Porn is more popular than ever.

But that doesn't mean all pornography is industry-created or industry-supplied. A professional grade digital video camera that cost $40,000 four years ago now goes for about $4,000. A webcam, a phone cam or even a pocket camera that can handle video as well as stills gives each of us the opportunity to star in our own erotic pictures. The difference between the sexual revolution 2.0 and the Polaroids of the 1980s is that it's so much easier to distribute homemade porn that consenting to appear in it at all is a huge sign of trust. Whether you plan to run for office someday or not, the risk you take in giving your lover permission to archive your naughty bits is that those pictures will end up online for all the world to see.

On the other hand, in a relationship based on trust—or exhibitionism—homemade porn is a logical couples activity. Just don't keep your movies in a place where the kids will find them.

Porn and a Room of Her Own

From what I've seen, online porn has much to offer us if we use it wisely. Because the more you think about sex, the more you want to have sex. And the more sex we have, the stronger our relationships become, because how can you stay mad at somebody who has to peel you off the ceiling in the morning?

OK, I know, I'm oversimplifying. But bear with me.

Online pornography is having widespread effects on our sex lives. Women in particular now have a safe and private place to look at sexually explicit images they would probably not have seen if they had to march into a porn shop to find them. And anyone who buys into the myth that women are not aroused by the visual would be surprised at just how many women are viewing online porn; more than one source suggests that 30 to 40 percent of visitors to adult websites are female.

I think our assumption that women aren't stimulated by sexual imagery arises from the fact that women tend to crave multi-sensory sexual experiences. We want the lighting, the scents, the music, the textures of the sheets or the grass beneath our backs, and, yes, the vision of our lover. Women often want *context*—hence the general (but not always accurate) assumption that a woman will reach for beautifully produced, plot-driven porn rather than wall-to-wall sex scenes.

I am not much of a solo porn viewer. I'd much rather use it with a lover, to add an element of naughtiness or to jump-start desire when one or both of us are too tired for sex. But like most newbies, I too was curious about online porn. In the mid-1990s I subscribed to a "gold key" service that handled the age verification process for adult webmasters. I believe the service cost 15 dollars a year, which bought an ID and password that let you enter any site that partnered with the credentialing company. I thought it was a good system; you only had to submit your credit card number to one place, rather than dozens of adult sites, and it seemed effective at keeping most unauthorized users out.

I found that what I liked about online porn was the opportunity to look, in secret, at people doing things I was curious about but had never tried. I looked at a lot of close-up anal sex in that first month. I also discovered a penchant for hot gay men *in flagrante delicto.* And I explored various sexual fetishes, discovering that my own comfort level with spanking and bondage is closer to "BDSM lite" than to anything that might scare the horses. Every preference, kink, fetish and fantasy has a website and often a community of people delighted to discover they're not alone in their desires. These days, there's even a community for asexuals—people who identify as one gender or another but who feel no sexual attraction at all to others. (If that's you, visit www.asexuality.org to find the understanding and support you've probably gone without most of your life.)

Now, I lived in San Francisco at the time, one of the last places on earth where anyone is going to persecute you for looking at dirty pictures. I could have gone down to the local newsstand and asked for recommendations and no one would have looked askance at me. In fact, I could have dressed up in pajamas, a cowboy hat, and a feather boa and asked for recommendations, and no one would blink an eye. That's one of the things that makes San Francisco such an interesting place to live.

One friend of mine found her ideas about porn changed dramatically after she finally went online and looked at it. Before, she assumed the women were beautiful and the men were not, and that every scene was inherently degrading to women. Yet spending the time to look at a variety of erotic content gave her a different perspective. Yes, some porn humiliates women. Some porn humiliates men. Some porn caters to those who like an element of humiliation in their sexual fantasies or experiences. Meanwhile, other porn just shows people having sex, without any deep considerations of how a 15-minute blow job affects society or women's place in the world. Sometimes a blow job is just a blow job.

One of my personal sexual fantasies consists of lying across a coffee table on my back, my hands wrapped around two different men's cocks, and my lips sealed around a third, while another man kneels between my thighs and yet another masturbates above my belly and breasts.

If an actress in a similar scene is degraded, and represents the humiliation of all women by all men, what does it say about me that imagining the scene makes me wet and achy? I do not feel shame or disgrace when I write the episode in my mind, and I do not interpret similar scenes in pornography as promoting the oppression of women.

What many women have discovered through online porn is that sex looks silly no matter who's doing it, and that bodies are after all just bodies. Porn stars have pimples and scars, weird bumps and birthmarks, cellulite and moles. The difference is they don't let such things stop them from feeling sexy. Every body type, shape, age, color and sexual orientation is represented in online porn. In fact, you'll find a lot more variation and "regular people" in adult entertainment than you do in mainstream movies and television.

Some women feel worse about their bodies after looking at porn, while others feel sexier and empowered by the experience. What's important is that we all, men and women, remember that porn is just porn. It's not a model for how all sex should be all the time. It's not a blueprint for intimacy, nor is it a medium on which to base our expectations about attractiveness, willingness or enthusiasm. It's simply another way to bring the erotic into our sex lives, in a way that women have historically been proscribed from doing.

And from what Sex Drive readers have told me, men think it's about time. Why should women have all the fun of plots and high production values? Why should men be the only ones allowed to enjoy sexual movies? Why shouldn't couples enjoy porn together as part of a varied and hot sex life?

Columnist Dana Harris summed up the "women and porn" question nicely in an article in *Variety*. Dana had posted an ad on Freecycle.com in order to get rid of several porn videos that were taking up too much space on the shelves. Within minutes she was receiving email from people willing to take the tapes off her hands. "My wife is going love these," said one man. Another explained he'd send the videos to his mom. Another respondent was a 50-year-old woman with salt-and-pepper dreadlocks.

I'm not going to indulge myself with a feminist rant about the pros and cons of pornography, although you can probably entice me into one if you come to the forums at www.reginalynn.com. I will leave it with this: some women like porn, some hate it, some remain neutral. Thanks to the internet, we now have the same opportunities as men to explore our responses to porn and to develop our own preferences. We can have informed opinions about where and whether it fits in our personal lives.

The more women look, the more we talk about it amongst ourselves. The more we talk about it, the more we demand what we want to see. The more demanding we get, the more influence we have over what and how porn gets produced.

Pornography To Go

I once provided an accidental peep show with my PDA on an airplane. This was back when color screens had just been introduced. I was playing strip poker on a red-eye flight, carefully angling the display away from my neighbors. About 10 minutes into the game, I realized that my screen was reflecting off the dark window and presenting a clear, magnified picture to anyone who cared to look. Whoopsiedoodle.

Now, mobile porn is the Next Big Thing in adult entertainment. Cell phones are ideal content receivers, as are PDAs and handhelds and PlayStation Portables (PSPs). We carry one or more of these gadgets with us everywhere we go, and we can send and receive data packets from just about anywhere, too. Despite dead zones—which for some reason seem to include my desk and my bed no matter what city I'm in—phone service is ubiquitous compared to wireless internet.

On the other hand, if you want to watch two or more people having sex, they have to be very small people to fit into a phone display. Handhelds have bigger screens, but even they hover around 2 x 3 inches. It makes me believe that the *idea* of having pornography with you wherever you go is even more exciting than viewing it. It's like having sex in a public place where you risk being discovered. Knowing that everyone around you is oblivious to your activity, going about their regular business, and yet just might catch you, can be a turn-on.

The whole point of a mobile phone is to escape the tyranny of the phone cord and talk while we're out and about. On the train, standing in line, walking down the strand at Venice Beach. That's the joy and the curse of cell phones—we use them in public. And while porn in public spaces may be part of the thrill for some, most of us prefer privacy. And you probably have a private space with a more porn-friendly technology like a computer or television.

Still, one Very Good Thing could come out of a successful porn-to-go industry. Think of how pornography ensured the success of the VCR and the DVD, not to mention high-speed internet access. Now imagine what adult content delivery to cell phones could mean for mobile phone consumers. Who wants to pay for airtime or use up minutes in addition to paying for naughty pictures? Not I. That business model has to go.

When video phones are cheap, data transmission is fast and airtime charges are a thing of the past, will we have the adult industry to thank? Maybe. Porn may be the catalyst for a paradigm shift in phone use, persuading the masses to associate phones with content as much as conversation.

But I think the real revolution here is not pornography at all. The killer app will take advantage of the essential function of a cell phone, a feature even more important than its mobility: the ability to connect people with other people. Cell phones are interactive and interpersonal. They aren't entertainment boxes waiting to receive content to display to a passive user. Until the mobile content industry finds a way to incorporate personal communication into its porn—perhaps with multi-player sex games or seamless cybersex—I don't see us spending a lot of money on it.

When I asked the Sex Drive forum whether anyone would pay for cell phone porn, most said no or not yet. Not unless it had a "unique twist that really made it stand out for phone," said one member. Another asked "Why pay a professional when there are so many enthusiastic amateurs?"

Excellent point.

Addiction? Or Growing Pain?

Americans have become obsessed with porn: viewing it, fearing it, judging it, even condemning it or defending it, often without having seen it. In the past few years, the mainstream media has jumped at the chance to play up the fear factor about porn on the internet. Child porn and porn addiction dominate the headlines, even as Jenna Jameson's memoir *How to Make Love Like a Porn Star: A Cautionary Tale* dominated the best-seller lists for weeks. A search through the Los Angeles Public Library periodical database results in hundreds of articles about the rising rates of porn and cybersex addiction since the late 1990s and the development of the web.

The past five years have seen a marked increase in unhealthy use of pornography, if mainstream media is to be believed. What surprises me is that this surprises anyone. Of *course* we're obsessed with porn. Sexual imagery is extremely powerful. It inspires our brains to release endorphins that arouse us and insist that we drop what we're doing and have sex *right now* in order to perpetuate the species. It also sells us Coors Lite beer, Calvin Klein clothing and Fanta soda pop. The only reason we weren't porn-crazed before the internet is that we had to risk social stigma to get our hands on the stuff. Husbands don't want their cars seen parked outside Joe's Smut Shack and wives don't want the mailman smirking about the plain brown wrapper.

I hate to use the phrase "porn addiction" because I am not a doctor and I am not qualified to make a diagnosis or otherwise label someone as an addict. But it seems to be the label we've applied to the overwhelming compulsion to watch porn, such that viewing porn becomes your top priority, taking precedence over work and family. It's certainly a cause for concern and possibly intervention. Addiction, whether to alcohol or drugs or reality TV, is not healthy for us or those who love us.

A home internet connection eliminates the social constraints that prevented the masses from developing unhealthy obsessions with porn. And people who would not have indulged their curiosity when they thought they could get caught now have free rein to look at whatever they want, whenever they want, often without having to identify themselves or pay for it.

But most people won't become addicted to online porn. And among those who develop an obsession with it, I figure that most manage to overcome it. Studies show that when a person gets a home internet connection for the first time, a period of intense usage and even depression can set in. But within two years, the person puts the internet in context. Not only does the depression lift, but people report they feel more connected to family and friends and happier than they did before they had the internet at home.

For those who cannot tear themselves away from online porn, that temporary period of obsession can easily last long enough to destroy a relationship. At first, the novelty of it keeps you going back; then the hobby develops into a habit, and you find yourself arranging the rest of your life around this sexually arousing pastime.

And then one day—hopefully before it's too late—you wake up, realize what you're doing, blush from head to toe with mortification, and resume your regular life. The sexual imagery or interaction that so held your attention has become humdrum and boring.

After all, the addiction itself is not necessarily enjoyable. Most of the time, if you're truly addicted, you feel anxious, ashamed, maybe a bit manic or frantic. The euphoria you experience while surfing for porn gets harder to achieve, and you're left feeling disappointed and silly.

One Sex Drive reader describes it this way:

> Addiction results from an inability to get one's fix at the desired moment. A satisfying experience is the result of many factors weighed in together, only some of which are contained in the online component of the experience. Too often, people tend to think of the internet as a shortcut to something that actually requires working on many levels. Good porn and good cyber are like good sex, they appeal to the senses and to the mind, mixing playfulness, seriousness, and even the odd drop of nostalgic tragedy into an intoxicating cocktail. Repeatedly experiencing half the fix, enough to remember that it can be great but only scraping the surface of the full potential, makes one come back repeatedly hoping for the whole thing and always walking away empty handed. I don't think it's because people are being satisfied by their experiences that they come back for them compulsively. Rather, they do so because

> they know how satisfying it can be, and has
> been, but have overstuffed themselves like
> children on cheap candies and can no longer
> appreciate the fine stuff when it comes
> their way.

I have already experienced the novelty of online sex—although for me, as for many women, the lure was cyber-sex, not porn—and come out relatively unscathed on the other side. My geek friends are in the same position: we had DSL way back in the last century, as soon as it became available in California, and we are probably still a few years ahead of the curve in our internet experiences. That doesn't mean we're living in a weird technosexual bubble. It does mean that we've been where the majority of inter-net users are now, and for us, porn is back to being just porn. In fact, we're so saturated with it, it's hardly even fun anymore. Bummer.

Addiction is complex. I certainly don't have the answers. A man who finds online porn more alluring than his real relationship is not a man I want to be in a relationship with, so if he's single, maybe a porn obses-sion helps keep him out of the dating pool. But a man who managed to keep a job, love a wife and raise a fam-ily before the internet, and who now risks everything because he can't stop looking at porn? It's a testament to how strong the human sexual imagination is, that we can replace the reality of sex with the fantasy of it. It's not even the fantasy of it, it's *digital representation* of the fan-tasy, through pictures and sound.

We don't have enough experience with internet porn to know whether addiction is more common than not; we don't yet know the average period of time a newbie's obsession with online porn lasts. Yet I strongly suspect that over the next five to 10 years we will see a decrease in the percentage of internet users addicted to online porn, and that the majority of adults will put porn in its proper place.

What we might see is an increase in addiction to cybersex. I've always thought the only way porn sites can compete is to offer the one thing no one else can offer: personality. Interacting with performers and with other subscribers creates an ongoing connection that results in a different experience every time, adding an element of novelty and suspense. That is where the real danger lies.

As Wendy posted to the Sex Drive forum:

> I've seen plenty of people destroy some aspect of their lives by being addicted to something. It's the addiction that's the issue, no matter what is being abused. When a person can't control themselves and gets lost, letting everything else in life drop away, that's the problem. It's all about moderation and balance.

The solution is simple, in concept if not in execution. If you can't cope with porn in moderation, don't dabble in it at all.

Porn and Politics

Any time you have more than one person in a room, you have politics. Even people who say they ignore politics, whether national or office, cannot help but be influenced and affected by the politicking that goes on around us. And like it or not, what goes on in Washington has ramifications for your sex life if you live in America. During president Bill Clinton's tenure, the Supreme Court decided that oral sex didn't count as sex, exactly, delighting conflicted teenagers everywhere and thrusting oral sex into the political spotlight. Clinton was also the president who signed the Child Online Protection Act (COPA) into law, which sets out several rules about how porn producers have to keep minors out of porn.

The battle between those who condemn all porn as evil and those who see it as an expression of free speech has raged for decades. In 2004, Congress allowed four anti-pornography crusaders to present testimony about the evils of internet porn. The stated point of the hearing was for Congress to determine whether to fund further studies into how pornography and porn addiction affect society. Even though no previous study has shown that pornography causes rape or child molestation or violence, none of those studies had the internet to contend with.

My guess is that such a study would reveal that online pornography no more causes porn addiction or pedophilia than wineries cause alcoholism. Porn is nothing new—humans have long sought to capture the erotic in our art and entertainment. There's an entire room of "oops, my boobie is showing" paintings at the Legion of Honor Museum of Fine Art in San Francisco. Many years before the MPAA ratings system, the very first movie kiss was exchanged in "The Kiss," back in 1896. Contemporaries panned the "unbridled kissing ... repeated thrice." The kiss lasts all of 15 seconds and is said to be the inspiration for subsequent film censorship.

However, when I read the transcripts of the hearing, I could barely contain my astonishment. The theories posited sound so outlandish, they do more to damage the speakers' contentions than support them.

In brief: the hearing concluded that because porn bypasses the cognitive speech-making part of the brain it is unprotected by the First Amendment, that porn turns men into rapists, and—my favorite—that porn releases damaging "erotoxins" into the bloodstream.

The main problem is that the witnesses confused "addiction to porn" with "existence of porn." But pornography did not become a gazillion-dollar industry on addiction alone. (The prohibitionists like to compare it to heroin, which can only be profitable for dealers when users become addicted. Yet for most of us, watching porn is more akin to watching football than injecting drugs. Absorbing, exciting and temporary.)

Yet like any addiction, when the substance in question is relatively harmless to most people, as porn seems to be, criminalizing that substance backfires. Porn, like alcohol, is an indulgence that I suspect the vast majority of people enjoy in moderation, in small doses, or not at all. And porn, like alcohol, is meant to be a treat for adults. In fact, everyone I've spoken with in the adult industry also supports the separation of children from adult content—that's why it's called adult content. (I find I don't even think of child porn as porn. It is child abuse, a depraved and sickening crime. Applying the same label we apply to images of consensual sex among adults trivializes the violence inherent to this form of child abuse.)

The panel's concern that the internet makes pornography much more available to children than it was in the good ol' days of the printing press is definitely a valid one. The sexual revolution 2.0 will have to include efforts to educate adults in how they can keep pornography away from children. We certainly have room to develop better content filters, age validation methods and other technologies that would make it harder for kids to find porn online. (If nothing else, just think of the generation of brilliant problem-solvers we'll create.) Perhaps Americans could take a cue from Europe, where TV gets racy late at night, and parents can choose whether to let their children view it.

Education is key for kids too; we adults need to take responsibility for teaching children that porn is not real sex. I'm not saying the sex is faked—but it's fantasy. Most pornographic material is not a model for how teens should go about exploring their budding sexuality.

A Sex Drive reader told me how one mom dealt with her son's porn bookmarks. I'm not sure how she discovered them, but she sat down with the boy and looked at the pictures with him. And she made comments along the way about how the pictures did or did not reflect the reality of her own sex life, how a particular photo was obviously faked because it couldn't really be anything but painful to do whatever it was showing otherwise, how in 20 years of sexual activity she had never felt drawn to do this or that. I imagine it was a lesson that kid will never forget.

As a whole, however, the witnesses in this particular hearing failed to inspire my confidence. While some of their concerns made sense—I mean really, who could argue that addiction is healthy?—some of their examples exposed the shaky foundation beneath their case. This may be good news to porn defenders but it doesn't bring us any closer to an honest assessment of the role internet porn will play in the years to come.

During his testimony, psychiatrist Jeffrey Satinover claimed porn "causes masturbation." Now, most people know that biology causes masturbation, and that it happens with or without props. We're born sexual beings—even infants masturbate, long before they can even say "free porn," much less Google it. Given the other challenges our country is facing, autoeroticism is hardly high on the list of threats to families or society. I'd hate to have to replace it with macrame just because a handful of people can't stand the thought that I might be taking longer showers than they deem necessary.

And it wouldn't hurt certain people to let go of their obsessive guilt and add this simple pleasure to their daily routine.

Dr. Satinover's concern about masturbation was hardly the worst of it, though. Dr. Mary Anne Layden stated that "the myth that women are sexually aroused by engaging in behaviors that are actually sexually pleasuring to men is a particularly narcissistic invention of the pornography industry."

Her testimony actually made me sad. Like many sexually enthusiastic women, I'm plenty aroused by fellatio and other "behaviors" that are "pleasuring to men." One of the ways you know you're having good sex is that both partners are aroused. It's not one person doing something to another person, but rather everyone involved is having a great time. Mutual sharing, mutual arousal, mutual pleasure. To believe that women aren't actually aroused, or to imply that we SHOULD NOT be aroused, by activities that also arouse men, is a particularly misogynistic mindset about sex, made all the worse when perpetuated by a woman.

Dr. Judith Reisman testified that police always find pornography when searching the homes of rapists and pedophiles, suggesting that viewing porn leads to committing crimes. I'm more inclined to believe that poverty, disenfranchisement, desperation, racism, drug addiction, child abuse, ignorance and gang mentality contribute more to serious crimes than pornography does. Otherwise, almost 100 percent of men, and probably 50 percent of women, would be out there raping and pillaging. The reason police find porn in the homes of suspected or confirmed rapists and pedophiles is that rapists and pedophiles tend to be men, and men are far more likely to collect porn than women. Not necessarily because they like it better, but because until the internet, it was much more difficult for women to get to it.

I'd like to know how many American households could make it through a thorough police search without adult content turning up, especially if that search extended to your internet browser cache? Of course most of us aren't subject to police searches, and therefore our collections remain private. And you never know—now that we can view porn on the internet, those closet collections of hardcopy might be less common than they were 10 years ago.

It seems to me if Congress were to fund an in-depth, scientifically valid, non-partisan study on porn's role in society, we could lay these fears to rest. The porn prohibitionists would have to stop inventing scare tactics to support their agenda, which is quite simply to make decisions for other adults who are more than capable of making decisions on their own. And the porn enthusiasts will have to quit denying that some people have an unhealthy response to the product, just like some people will become alcoholics while others simply enjoy wine.

One encouraging message did come out of this hearing. Senator Jim Brownback (R-Kansas), who presided over the hearing, told the press that he has "friends" who limit the time they spend alone in hotel rooms in order to avoid the temptation of pay-per-view porn. I'm going to take it on faith that PPV porn is tempting, having never felt the urge to order it myself. But what the senator is saying is that these friends are taking control of their own decisions about adult content. They know it's a temptation for them, they know they don't really want to see it, and so they avoid putting themselves in situations where they might compromise their decisions not to view porn at all. If they can set and follow their own limits, why can't the rest of us?

Exactly.

Why Online Porn Matters

I live within an hour's drive of Chatsworth, California, the porn capital of America. I've attended adult industry trade shows and conventions, and I've talked with talent and with the folks behind the cameras. Not every actress is exploited, not every performer is desperate, and not every viewer is an addict. In fact, the majority of industry and consumers are simply people who get up, go to work, come home, hang out with their families, enjoy some titillating entertainment, and go to bed.

Part of the sexual revolution 2.0 is the mainstreaming of pornography, and the eroticizing of the mainstream. Television has pushed the boundaries since the advent of HBO; the internet blasts through what's left.

Traditional broadcasters should watch AdultInternet.TV very closely, for the business model if not the content. AdultInternet.TV is the first adult internet-only television channel, complete with regular shows and an advertising-based business model. Cartoons, cooking demonstrations, news, reality shows—any genre you find on broadcast, you'll find at this website. What happens here will help define the future of entertainment content delivery, especially as the audience develops expectations for what internet TV should look like.

For lovers, porn can be a way to open up discussion about subjects you're otherwise embarrassed to mention to your partner. It can enable couples to explore sexual activities that one partner wants to try but the other doesn't.

It can put you at ease with your silliest fetish and make man-on-top missionary position seem exotic again, because after trying all the positions you'll see in online porn, it's a relief to return to something so simple.

Most of us have more important things to do than to bother obsessing about online porn. Yet more and more, couples are incorporating pornography into their sexual toolboxes. Nothing like a "couples movie" to transition the mood from the working, parenting, bill paying, household chore modes that dominate a modern couple's life.

Online porn may be scaring more than the horses, but its effect on modern relationships should not be dreaded. As accessible porn helps both men and women become more comfortable talking to each other about sex, we're also going to become more comfortable asking for what we want, finding partners who suit us, and creating the sex lives we thought other people were having without us. Online porn is actually facilitating a new, more relaxed attitude about sex among people who use porn as it is meant to be used.

We are experiencing growing pains as we attempt to handle the sudden onslaught of sexual imagery. Porn addiction is a part of that. So is the sexualizing of mainstream media, and the backlash against all of it.

Talking About the Revolution

Join us at www.reginalynn.com to discuss how online porn affects our sex lives.

What has watching porn taught you about your body, your sexuality?

Do you think the adult entertainment industry should be regulated, and if so, how extensively and by whom?

Have you experienced any negative effects from online porn? What positive consequences have you observed?

REVOLUTIONARY PROFILE
Carly Milne

Carly Milne writes Pornblography.com and owns Sin Spin, a publicity firm for the adult entertainment industry. She is the editor of Naked Ambition (Carroll & Graf, Fall 2005), an anthology in which dozens of prominent women involved in adult entertainment share their ideas, experiences, histories and passions to help us understand how porn has helped a generation of women claim their sexual selves on their own terms.

Tell me something about how online porn affects relationships.

I definitely believe online porn has an effect, and it's a positive one. The advent of internet porn has made sexuality choices more comfortable for people. You don't have to go to the video store, slip into a secret room to pick out your movie, and then try to hide it in between a Disney film and a Roman Polanski feature. You can sit at home where no one will know, no one will see, and you can get your jollies. In that respect, internet porn has really helped people become more in touch with sexuality. There isn't that stigma to doing it, your neighbors and your pastor aren't going to "catch" you. Sexuality is private anyway, and the option to have porn in your own home makes it much more convenient and comfortable.

Some say that's the problem, that porn has become so accessible it is destroying relationships and families.

When something becomes that readily available, some people will take advantage of it. I think it takes a strong individual to disallow it—whatever it is, drugs, alcohol, porn—from running their lives. People who are socially inept, or insecure, or not happy with themselves, can retreat to this world of internet porn where girls are always available to them and will do whatever they want them to. These people end up building a fantasy life in their head, because that's easier than going out and talking to a flesh and blood human being. And I think that's where internet porn gets its stigma—people propel themselves to become addicted to it, and that's where it winds up hurting relationships.

And those people can't be fixed. They have to fix themselves.

The internet and technology are bringing humans to a new level in our sexual explorations. How we meet, how we find a partner, how we conduct our sex lives are all changing. How does internet porn fit into that?

Women, if they are comfortable enough in themselves and do not look at porn and say, "Oh my God I don't have breasts like that, I don't have thighs like that," generally become more adventurous sexually. They're more likely to say, "Wow, that looks like fun; hey honey, let's try it." Internet porn can open up lines of communication.

I don't think there's been as much of a change for men, although in general terms, obviously it's a lot more convenient. Men who are in relationships tend to become more open to communication about sex as well.

Overall, we're talking about porn and sex a lot more openly than in the past. Really, there's no subject like porn to get people riled up and talking. Secondary would be religion, but I think that's a far, far distant second. People are way more excited discussing sex and porn than they are on any other subject.

Does internet porn have an affect on how we view our bodies, our sexuality?

Most astute women who watch porn will notice that the porn girls do have stretch marks, pooches, cellulite. They aren't perfect like on the airbrushed covers. Porn can do a lot to teach self-esteem about bodies, especially when there's such a vast array of women's bodies in adult entertainment. Women should feel more comfortable after dipping into internet porn, rather than insecure.

Do women and men respond differently to porn, now that we have dispelled the myth that women aren't turned on by visual stimuli?

I think it makes women more adventurous, in a way, and while not necessarily more verbal, it makes them more communicative. Women are more readily open to using porn as a learning tool as opposed to an escape. Men are more drawn to using it as an escape than women are.

What is the main change you see now that we have online porn, rather than just mail-order or rental videos?

Internet porn has done a lot to make women more comfortable with porn. The one thing men take for granted as porn consumers is being comfortable—well, comfortable enough—with going out to a store to pick up a video like "Young Ripe Melons." They don't take into account that when a woman goes into a store, the majority of men, not all of course, but most of the men there tend to be of the raincoat or semi-fiendish type. Of course, not at stores like Blowfish or Good Vibrations, but let's say you're in a city without a "clean, well-lighted" sex store, or it's a major trek to go to the local mom and pop adult outlet. And Joe Blow with his raincoat and his hardcore gonzo sees you in the porn section. He's automatically going to think you're ready to bend over for him right there, because clearly if you're a chick who's into porn, you must be way into everything including him. It's a *very* creepy vibe.

That's why we don't have conclusive numbers about how much porn women view, when women are more comfortable going online or borrowing from a boyfriend. And internet porn has done a lot to give women a comfort level they always sought—call it whatever you want, erotica, soft core, whatever, it's still porn, and we're equally as turned on as everyone else. Go ahead and wrap it in a story if that makes you feel better, but the bottom line is we are equally as turned on by the visual. But

until the internet we weren't as able to go after it because we
had to put ourselves in uncomfortable situations to get it.

So porn isn't all evil?

I've always said that porn of any kind is like a condiment.
You wouldn't eat an entire bowl of mustard. That's not filling. If
you have a healthy sex life, be it with a monogamous partner or
with a number of people you're dating, or whatever your choice,
porn can be something that can help you express yourself. It can
help you reach a greater understanding and comfort level with
your significant other (or whoever you're banging that week).

But if you are in that mindset where you're going to turn
around and constantly be consuming porn, if you're going to
take yourself out of reality to the point where you start thinking
girls should act like this all the time, and if not there's something wrong with them, you have a problem. But it's your problem, not the internet's problem.

5

Real Sex: Finding True Love, or at Least the Possibility of Dinner, Online

My experience with online dating is fairly typical. I created an online profile through Salon.com. I invested some time writing essays that avoided the standard clichés but tried to convey a sense of who I am. I uploaded a flattering picture but warned readers that I was seldom that glamorous and not to get their hopes up.

I was also honest about what I was and wasn't looking for. I was not shopping for a boyfriend or a husband. I was dating for the first time in my adult life, and I just wanted to be open to the experience, without an End Goal. As it turned out, I met several good men who will make other women very happy someday. I went on a few dates that belong in the "are you *kidding*?" hall of fame, and agreed to go steady with a professor who turned out to be—well, you can read about him in the Eternal Sunshine chapter. Overall, my experience was positive, and probably fairly typical for a woman not seeking her One True Love.

Last century, only nerds and losers fell in love over the internet. The uninitiated asked, with smug faces, "How could anyone get to know anyone through a computer? Everyone on the internet is lying about who they are anyway."

Then online personals entered the scene. Within five years, the stigma attached to meeting on the internet gave way to the cachet of online dating. It was no longer "Weird, you met online?" Now it was "Which online dating sites do you recommend?" Even the authors of *The Rules*, a book that counseled a return to an earlier era of dating etiquette, acknowledged this new realm with a sequel: *The Rules for Online Dating*.

Dating by database has huge potential to redefine relationships and how we find them in the sexual revolution 2.0. We have built a new set of expectations about the dating life and what we want to get out of it.

If you've taken the plunge, you probably know that a dating site exists for everyone. Match.com and Yahoo Personals are the most mainstream; SpringStreetNetworks, accessible through mostly alternative media such as Nerve.com and Salon.com, has the most indie-intellectual types who are as likely to be after booty calls as true love; BikerKiss.com and DateMyPet.com connect motorcycle enthusiasts and pet lovers, respectively. AdultFriend Finder.com makes no bones about its purpose, which is to connect people with others for sex. Yes, swinging is as alive and well as it was in the 1970s, only this time you are not limited by geography. Everyone who posts a profile at AFF says exactly what they're looking for, eliminating the need to scope out someone's interest in a subtle and possibly offensive way. Explicit photos and anything goes profiles let you accept or reject people without hurting their feelings, so everyone's happy.

Online personals started out as a phenomenon of the young, but by 2004, seniors were the fastest growing demographic for online dating. Of course, on the internet, you're a senior the day you turn 40, but even so, many 60-somethings began finding new love through sites like SeniorFriendFinder.com and eHarmony.com. One reader reported that two years after telling him that meeting people online was strange and possibly dangerous, his 63-year-old mother could hardly keep track of her internet suitors.

Dating used to be a means to an end, not a lifestyle. It still is, for some, but that end ranges widely, from marriage and parenthood . . . to someone to hang out with . . . to sex. And for more people than admit it, dating has become an activity in itself. With so many millions of profiles to choose from, why limit yourself to just one? But even when sex (virtual, if not actual) is available any time you want it (if you know where to look), most people eventually want something more. Even in the sexual revolution 2.0, it's not all about sex all the time.

My mom always said the best way to find love is to participate in activities you enjoy, with other people who enjoy them. Sierra Club hikes, volunteer clean-up days at the beach, ceramics classes, salsa lessons and dog parks are all places where singles not only have a place to congregate, they have a reason for being there and something to talk about. My mom's wisdom still applies in the internet age. In fact, that is the internet's greatest contribution to the search for love: the ability to find other people who share your interests, no matter how obscure or mainstream those interests are.

Some people will never be comfortable with online dating, not because they think dating is silly (it is, but so what?) but because they can't imagine starting a relationship over the computer. But that's not what internet dating is. The computer, like most of the technology of the sexual revolution 2.0, is only the tool that brings you together. In fact, one mistake many of us make when we first start exploring online personals is to spend too much time communicating by computer before a first date. This probably sounds odd coming from me, but I learned that too much pre-date email and IM can backfire in an online dating context. Either you fall for each other so completely online that you ignore the violently flapping red flags of your first date, or you set yourself up for a huge disappointment when you aren't nearly as compatible or similar in real life as you were in text. If your initial volley of e-talk inspires you to meet, go have that half-hour coffee date. If that goes well, then come back and get personal in email and IM.

It's strange that too much chat can bad for online dating when it seems to create strong relationships between people who meet online in other venues like chat rooms, forums and discussion groups. The difference is that the relationships that grow out of the latter contexts are often surprises, unintentional, not the original goal of the couple. Online dating by definition involves real-world interaction and—for most—the hope of a real-world relationship. The expectations are higher in a dating situation.

Love Without Borders

Whether through online dating sites or other communities, the internet makes the obstacles of time and distance more of an inconvenience than an impossibility. Connecting with so many people in so many time zones and so many geographical locations makes us more aware that we are not necessarily the center of the universe. When you're just looking for community, it doesn't tend to matter where your favorite people in the group live. If you begin to form bonds with one person, exchanging email and instant messages outside the group, well, it's hardly your fault if you live 800 miles apart. And if that connection eventually evolves into love, it is not beyond the pale to plan for one or both of you to move if you decide to get married.

Falling in love like that is a surprise. With online personals, you don't have to put up with the surprises of distance. You can search for dates within five, 10, or 50 miles of your zip code. Or you can choose a city—yours or one you'd like to visit—and look for matches there. I generally set my preferences for "within 500 miles," because I live in both Los Angeles and San Francisco and it is about 400 miles from my southern door to my northern one. If I'm willing to travel, why limit the search to the city where I spend only 70 percent of my time?

For city folk, online dating has been dubbed the extreme sport of the decade. It makes it possible for busy professionals to look for love, a night out or sex beyond the borders of their own social and professional circle. Why take chances with strangers in bars or produce aisles when you can read someone's profile, exchange email and talk on the phone—all before you decide whether to go on a date? You never know if people in bars have anything in common with you other than being at that club at that time, perhaps enjoying the music and scene and perhaps not. Peruse an online personal and you find out quite a lot about a stranger, in what he picks to write and what he doesn't, in the films and books he picks for his Top 5, or the detail in which she describes her pets.

The real boon of online personals, though, is not the ability to help 20- and 30-something white collars get laid (although once when I explained the concept of this book to a 24-year-old at a seminar, he got excited and wanted to tell me all about how he and his buddy "bang chicks off the internet"). As I see it, the most valuable contribution to society database dating is making is its ability to bring together folks who would not ordinarily meet each other at all.

A divorced man who shares custody of his three children cannot move away from his small town in search of new beginnings—not without abandoning his kids, and what woman wants a boyfriend who would do that? Yet when the population is 4,000 and you've already met the other 49 single people, the possibilities can look awfully bleak. With online dating, those constraints disappear. You could spend every weekend exploring the singles scene in the nearest city, debating over when and how to reveal where you really live and the fact that you have kids (in which case how can you spend so much time in the city?)—or you can stay home, state those conditions in your profile, and let only those who are fine with that configuration contact you. You can take your time getting to know people before you ever attempt a first date. You might have to drive 150 miles to spend half an hour at a Starbucks, but it's worth it because you've been able to get to know her a little bit first, and she already knows where you live and that your first priority is staying close to your kids.

Online dating solves the issue for those too shy to approach people in person, whether at Sierra Club volunteer days or at karaoke night in the local dive. It gives people with "alternative lifestyles" or obscure fetishes a chance not only to find other people who share those interests, but to find them in a setting where everyone is clearly looking for connections.

In other words, finding love is challenging enough—any tool that can help bring us together can only be A Good Thing. Think of what might happen when lovers who 10 years ago would never have been able to find each other actually reach out and fall in love and perhaps even have children. A city girl might find out she loves living in a town of 4,000. A man who never left the town he grew up in might finally go on a date with someone who didn't know he was the one whose boxers were run up the flagpole in ninth grade.

I know it's not as easy as all that. I had dates that made me cringe for a year afterward, dates with men who seemed enamored of me during dinner but never contacted me again, and dates with people I liked but could never see myself sleeping with. A disastrous turn around the dance floor with one date resulted in his telling me, right there in the middle of the bar, that if we weren't compatible in the two-step we weren't going to be compatible at anything else and we should call it a night. I think he was surprised at my eager handshake and "thank you, good night"—he must not have realized that I had been thinking the same thing, I just hadn't worked out how to say it yet. But at least I discovered a great country bar.

Nothing important is easy. Finding a great job takes time and effort. Getting your first novel published can take the fortitude to stick with it through 100 rejections. Turning a puppy into a great dog requires sleepless nights and consistent effort for more than a year; keeping him a great dog requires a lifetime commitment. Online dating may not always be easy, but it sure does break down barriers that would have made it even harder to find love, pre-internet.

And you know something else? Let's say you don't find true love through online dating, and you're tired of eating at restaurants or meeting for coffee and telling the same stories, answering the same questions, that come up on every first date. Your horizons have still been expanded. Every person you meet teaches you something about yourself. Sometimes you learn that you need to make some changes, or that your ideas about what makes a person attractive have evolved. Perhaps you will discover prejudices you didn't know you had. Or someone will introduce you to the joys of bowling, Anime, in-line skating or even line dancing. Even if the relationship doesn't work out, you have been enriched by the experience.

Leveling the Playing (or is that Player?) Field

I hate the phrase "casual sex" because there's nothing casual about sex. I don't care if it's a one-night-stand or a strict schedule of booty buddies—sex creates connections and obligations ("strings"), whether we want it to or not. That doesn't mean that I believe sex belongs only within a monogamous, Christian marriage. And for women like me who struggle against the cultural assumption of marriage and monogamy, but who cannot be dismissed with "boys will be boys," online dating has given us the tools to lead the kind of sex lives the boys always said they wanted to have.

Despite the women's movement and the advances we have made toward gender equality in the corporate workplace, it seems that many women still hesitate to make the first move. Dr. Janet Lever checks regularly with her students, finding that even today, most young women say they feel uncomfortable asking men out in person.

But online, the rules change. Women not only make the first move, they can set parameters that previously were thought to be the prerogative of men. It's usually easier for a woman to find sex than it is for a man. All we have to do is walk into a crowded place and yell out "I'll have sex with the first one who buys me a drink." Of course, most of us have standards, which makes it more challenging to find a suitable partner, whether for short- or long-term involvement.

As I write this, I'm seeing a wonderful man, who has patiently stuck it out despite my frequent traveling, the emotional roller coaster of writing a book, and the fact that I am willing to reveal any detail about my private life if it helps me make a point or put readers at ease. But for a few years in my late 20s and early 30s, I had a harem. That is, I would see one man fairly regularly (about once a week) and a few others who would cycle in and out (no pun intended). Most of the occasionals lived in other cities, which made it easier to manage and to avoid running into one while out with another.

Everything was out in the open. Not that I introduced them to each other or mentioned who or how many I was seeing—only that I wasn't exclusive, and I didn't expect them to be either. Juggling that many dates was exhilarating at times, exhausting at others, often both. But it was motivating, too. I ran almost every day, I ate well, I flossed daily, I wore glitter on my cheekbones. And always, always, *always* practiced safe sex. No condom, no action, period.

I was always up front about what I was looking for. Some fun, some sex, some laughs, but not falling in love. The guys liked this at first, thinking they'd at last met their dream girl. All the sex and flirting, none of the commitment, right? But after a while, it began to bother them. One by one, they moved on, either to pursue a steady relationship with another woman or to be free to find one. One in particular couldn't stand the idea that I might be going to bed with someone else; this was ironic because he was the one who was most vocal about his need for "space" and "freedom."

I'm still friends with a couple of the men I met during those times, but most of them have gracefully—and graciously—fallen out of touch.

I know I'm making it sound like I had entire battalions on rotation through my bed. Not true. But it wasn't your old-fashioned single-woman-seeks-husband situation either. I didn't go on a few dates with a guy, sleep with him, and then become his girlfriend. I didn't go out with a man two or 10 times, decide he wasn't The One, and move on to the next.

Through the internet, I could pre-screen prospective dates well enough to get a good idea of whether we'd hit it off in person. I could tell them what they were getting into, giving them a graceful way out if they weren't into it. I embarrassed some with my directness, but I wanted to avoid misunderstandings as much as possible. Sex no matter how "casual" creates bonds. If you're going to be polyamorous, you should be up front about it.

And meanwhile, I had my dog, my friends, my career, my day-to-day life. I didn't need a man to provide a home, car or children for me. The "traditional" relationship pattern—find boyfriend, get married, have children, occasionally envy single friends—simply didn't apply. Financial support, I provide for myself. Emotional support came from strong friendships. What I really wanted from a man was flirtation and chemistry, conversation and sex.

In short, I had the kind of dating life men have historically been allowed, even expected, to have. The kind a red-blooded American male is supposed to *want* to have, even if he doesn't really.

Database dating levels the playing field. Women can live like bachelors and enjoy it as much or more than men do. We can say so right in our online dating profiles to weed out the unsuitable. Change of heart? Edit the profile.

In my experience and observation, women are just as capable as men at non-exclusive dating. I would venture to say that we're even more suited to it, because we have such deep friendships with other women (and often men). We have the support system in place to provide companionship and emotional stability outside of our sex life, while many men often find this only through their girlfriends or wives.

I remember a discussion I had one night while out to dinner with a dozen women writers, half of whom write about sex and relationships. Someone mentioned a couple she knew who was struggling with their relationship. "He wants it to be 'open' so they can sleep with other people but still be primary partners," she said. A collective gasp halted all simultaneous conversations, and my friend Joyce put into words what we were all thinking. "The *man* is asking for polyamory? That *never* happens!"

In my case, the men who were most insistent that they could handle and in fact preferred the absence of a monogamous relationship turned out to be the ones most likely to fall in love with me, to break their hearts yearning for something they thought they wanted. (When you're seeing more than one person you tend to show only your best to each one, and to turn to friends in times of sorrow or need. Consequently, they form an idealistic image of you as the Perfect Girlfriend.)

These are the men who ended up hurt or angry. Perhaps they were unsure of their roles, hanging out with a self-sufficient woman who made no secret of her intent to remain solo. Or perhaps they just got jealous, possessive. Either way, it made for a few awkward conversations, and attempts on my part to be even more direct and clear next time. And eventually I gave it all up, took a hiatus from dating, and had a wonderful time dating myself. (Naturally, six months later, The Boyfriend wandered into my life, just when I had everything exactly the way I wanted it. What's a girl to do?)

It's all part of the Brave New World of Internet Dating, at least for urban 30-somethings hooked in to the online catalog. We may not have invented the idea of open relationships, sex on the first or second date, or sexual freedom. But we're the first generation of adults who witnessed the demise of our parents' marriages in large numbers, and the first grown-ups who had several databases to choose from when looking for sex and love.

In my entirely unscientific study in the early days of Sex Drive, I discovered a strong sense of "boyfriends come and go but girlfriends are forever" among my female contemporaries. One lover can't handle it, move on to the next. If you get tired of it, find someone special enough and quit shopping. Above all, keep your tribe strong. And use condoms.

I don't think this is a permanent lifestyle for most people, although for many women, finally having the tools in place to support a polyamorous life may lead to some epiphanies. One close friend, after finally leaving an abusive relationship, found that online dating woke up a part of her that had gone dormant years earlier. All it took were emails from interested parties. She went on a few dates, but polyandry has never been her style, not even in fantasy. Before long she decided it wasn't for her and she began to disengage from internet dating to focus on getting her life in order. Of course, that's the day she met her match (a keeper if I ever met one, but don't tell him I said so—it's still too soon for comments like that).

For most, managing multiple dates eventually becomes exhausting, even for those of us who do not prefer monogamy but who respect the commitment when we give it. The important thing is that the internet gives both men and women more choices about how to conduct their love lives. It gives us the freedom to figure out what, and who, we ultimately want. And it gives us the tools to find people who want the same kinds of things.

Next, Please

One thing about online dating is that you very quickly develop a catalog mentality. Even before you make contact with anybody, you click through profile after profile and—in the beginning at least—there seems no end to the number of potentials. And with every date that doesn't lead to another, you can console yourself with the fact that there's another waiting on the next page.

This isn't necessarily a bad thing. It can protect you from staying with someone just because you'd rather have someone than no one, not because it's someone who is good for you. It can keep your spirits up when someone you really, really liked brings out the "there's just no chemistry" or "I just told this other person I would stop seeing other people" speech. And it can open your eyes to the possibilities so you can hone your profile to reflect you, and your ideal mate, better.

The flip side of course is that for a generation who saw marriages split, custody battles rage and parents date, a catalog mentality can make it that much harder to commit to one person. You can get so wrapped up in falling in love that you forget that love, over the long term, takes work. At the first sign of disharmony, it's possible now to bolt, because lurking in the dark corner of your mind is the knowledge that a big database of other lovers is waiting out there. Even just entering a more settled stage, when the sex becomes more intimate but less dramatic, can push some people to look for the next great passion. And because the people you meet through online dating are usually not members of your immediate circle, your friends don't have to know how many hearts you're breaking, or how many times you're going out with people obviously wrong for you.

Oddly enough, after living in Los Angeles as long as I have, I still believe most people have good sense. Yet the catalog mindset is insidious precisely because it seems like common sense. No matter how much you like a person you've met through online personals, you always know all you have to do is click to the next page. You might get tired, bored or frustrated with "the whole dating thing"—and many do—but absolute heartbreak is less common, because you have so many other options. Often, it's that overwhelming number of options turning out to be not so desirable that turns us off dating altogether. (Which of course can lead to Falling in Love. There's a reason that it has become cliche to find someone when you're no longer looking. I imagine this is because when you truly let go of the need to search, you settle into being just you. That is, you are no longer attempting to be someone, or to project someone that you think someone else is looking for. And that's when the people who best match you are going to notice you, whether online, offline or somewhere in between.)

As long as you don't set your standards and expectations so high that no person could ever possibly satisfy you, dating by the database helps you discover your likes and dislikes, what you can tolerate and what you can't, and even some truths about yourself (some more comfortable than others). I discovered that I have a high tolerance for personality quirks that my girlfriends find, well, odd, as long as the man possessing said quirks is *interesting*. Same goes for looks. If a man looks interesting, perhaps because of a birthmark or a long crooked nose (mmmm) or amazing eyes in an otherwise homely face, I will find him attractive as long as his personality is also interesting. And I learned I'm a shy man's dream date, as I seem to be able to put him at ease long before the end of the date. But then I get bored and even resentful when I'm cast in the role of teacher, social director or entertainer. When I finally figured this out I stopped going out with painfully shy men because it didn't seem fair to set someone up for me to become irritated at him.

The problem with a catalog of dates is that we do tend to develop unrealistic expectations. When you can describe who you're looking for right down to his eye color, you can unintentionally build a mental picture of the "perfect" one for you—and when a date doesn't immediately fit this expectation, you cut him or her off before anything has a chance to develop. And if you do get into a relationship with someone, the first time it starts to get difficult, with a disagreement or a fight or just one of those inevitable quirks, it's all too easy to avoid working on the relationship and just head back to the catalog, where you start over on the same story but with a different co-star.

The catalog is fine up to a certain extent. It's when you're committing to a life partner that you have to take the chance and love as if the entire inventory has been sold out—and you got the best one.

Why Real Sex Matters

Someone once said that every generation thinks it invented sex. Obviously, we didn't, or we wouldn't be here. But we have invented a new way to find people to have sex with, reaching out beyond our geographical boundaries and our personal tribes. Every couple who meets through the internet forms another connection for all of us. Even people who part ways after a few dates bring their combined experiences, connections and assumptions to the meeting and both leave changed by the experience.

How could this not change the world? Subtle at first, yes, but look at everything we're doing that's based on our new connections. We're developing ways to have remote sex. We're embedding multiple communication methods in all of our gadgets. My cell phone can send and receive text, still pictures and video (with audio), and it even lets me talk to people in real time just like the earliest telephones in the last century.

Real sex sometimes produces real children. Think of how the next generations will grow up, born from parents who fell in love despite long distances, despite differences in culture and upbringing, because of the meeting of minds they found online. Will these children reject the prejudices that hampered previous generations? Will these children wonder why anyone ever thought it was so novel to have sex with people of different colors, traditions, backgrounds?

If you have preferences, kinks, fetishes or desires that you cannot afford to expose in your real world community, the internet is a godsend. You can find real sex with kindred spirits, without anyone in your immediate environment suspecting. Eventually, as more people form more connections in this clandestine manner, we may find that the need for secrecy slowly fades. How can it remain secret if everybody is doing it?

Talking About the Revolution

Come to www.reginalynn.com to talk about online dating in the forums.

Would you consider multiple lovers if you could screen them first? What has online dating taught you about your relationship preferences?

Will online dating become the default, most common way to meet one's match?

Have you fallen in love with someone you never would have met if not for the internet?

REVOLUTIONARY PROFILE
Evan Katz

Since 2001, Evan Katz has worked with thousands of people to help them create online personals that reflect who they truly are, rather than relying on the tired clichés everyone else uses. He is the founder of E-Cyrano.com and the author of I Can't Believe I'm Buying This Book: A Commonsense Guide to Internet Dating.

Is online dating changing the world?

Yes. It's changed my world. If online dating empowers someone to meet a kindred spirit with whom they never would have interacted in their normal life circumstance, it's a boon for everybody. So apart from the thousands upon thousands of anecdotal success stories about marriages that have resulted from online dating, think about how it has given people a voice and friendships and the ability to connect with each other.

People whose lives are being changed the most are people who are over 40, who don't have a tolerance for picking up strangers at bars, who may be divorced, who have kids to take care of. Online dating brings the equivalent of the singles scene into the home. You can still be social without having to go out.

I have to think it's a net positive for the world.

What do you think of the combination of dating with cybersex?

Was it ever separate?

I don't think Match.com is advertising itself as a place to meet people while remote-controlling their vibrators over the internet.

Wildly creative. What will they think of next? If there's a market for strangers controlling your vibrator, God bless you. As long as nobody's getting hurt by it, it's fine.

That's the thing with the internet as a whole—it has legit-imized and mainstreamed things that people would otherwise think of as really odd fetishes. Maybe there are still odd fetishes out there, but at least there's a community of people who share them now.

Where do you see online dating going in the future?

I think it's going to be ubiquitous, and we won't have the chatter or controversy or discussion that surrounds it even now. There was a time when only one person on the block had a TV, and everyone came over to watch TV together. We're already past the point where everybody says, "I know someone who dates online." Half of single America has dabbled in it, which only portends a bright future.

How do you address skepticism from people who worry about online dating?

Most of the skepticism is directed at me rather than at online dating. It's more like "How are you an expert, you're still single"—but frankly, I'm more likely to trust someone who's single and dating online than someone who's been married for 20 years.

Most people have computers, most people want to fall in love, and most people want to have sex, and by combining these elements you have a way of organically searching for whatever it is that you need. You end up connecting with people who may be from one apartment over or maybe the world over. It serves that mutual, undeniable need for connection.

Give us some advice for success—however a person defines that—in online dating.

Don't quit. Sometimes it's frustrating. You're not meeting the right people, you're going on bad dates. Hopefully you can learn from it all and minimize the bad experiences and maximize the good ones. That's what E-Cyrano is for. To give people the tools to figure out why this hasn't been working out for you, what are you doing wrong, and to fix it.

If you're looking for love you should put a major effort into this. If you're going to do it, make it count. If you're going to dabble, it's not going to do much good. It's like a gym membership. It's not always easy, it's sometimes painful, but there are vast rewards if you can integrate it into your life.

6

Would You Like to Play a Game?

When I was a kid, I used to play The Legend of Zelda with my brother. He'd work the controller, I'd sit next to him, and we'd make decisions about the game play together. I still don't have the patience to master the controls, but on and off through the years I've dipped into gaming, usually as a social activity with a friend.

Computer games are no longer restricted to a small cadre of uber-geeks. Video games have an annual revenue of about $10 billion, surpassing Hollywood's yearly take. (Not so surprising when you compare the prices. Game, $50. Movie ticket, $10. Time spent not thinking about work, priceless.)

People wring their hands over how much time kids spend playing computer games, perhaps without realizing that most gamers are in their 20s and 30s. According to the Entertainment Software Association, 94 percent of computer game buyers are over the age of 18. The average age of video and computer gamers is 30. And almost 40 percent of gamers are women.

I don't have time to play the games I'd like to play, but more and more, computer games are creeping into my consciousness. I have friends so hooked on one game or another that they forget to eat. Sex Drive's first publisher, TechTV, was assimilated by a television network all about gaming. *Playboy* got into the game with an October 2004 pictorial featuring four digital babes, characters from popular games, in various states of undress. And when I wrote a column asking where all the good cybersex had gone, role-playing games were the most popular answer.

Harald, a Sex Drive reader in Austria, wrote to tell me about his experience with World of Warcraft, a massive multiplayer online role-playing game, or MMPORG. Harald's words echo the vast majority of conversations I have had with MMORPG fans:

> I really appreciated the above average participation, interest, love for detail and general quality I encountered. Far from any generic banter or rude behavior, I met people who put a lot of energy into building relationships with imagined characters, going through all the stages from first tentative chatter up to very personal things. Even the humor isn't missing.

I'm not surprised at how popular games are. Computer games, particularly online games in which you interact with other players, let us play dress-up and pretend like nothing else. When was the last time you got to drop all the constraints of daily life and have a daring adventure? In a game, you can be another gender, another species, another person altogether. A man can learn what it's like to be a peasant woman working in a tavern; a woman can be a warrior princess to rival Xena. Male and female Sex Drive readers have written to me about the differing receptions they get when they enter role-playing games as one gender or another. Male characters tend to flirt with female characters, which is as one probably expects. But one woman reports that when she's female in the game, the male characters often get protective if she starts getting harassed by other players. It's not as overt as stepping in front of her and beating the other characters off, but they will support and join in with her efforts to tell off the jerks. When she enters the game as a male, she is treated as a rival by some males and as a boon companion by others, and she is flirted with by female characters.

Because role-playing games depend on building relationships with other players, it is not uncommon for players to forge friendships, have cybersex or even fall in love both inside and outside the game world.

Fantastic Fantasy

The best long-term games, like the best long-term sex, include strong elements of fantasy and recreation. For gamers, MMPORGs like EverQuest, Second Life or World of Warcraft are enough to stimulate the imagination and offer respite from the demands of the real world. My best analogy, for those who have never played a role-playing game, is that it's like interactive reading and storytelling. I may not be a hardcore gamer but I know the feeling it gives you. I've never found anything as powerful as a fantasy quest to put a technical or creative job into perspective. No looming deadline could compare to the horror of Sauron's tower of Barad-Dur. And no matter how impossible your boss's or client's demands, at least you're not trudging barefoot through Mordor with the fate of the world hanging from a chain around your neck.

If your imagination has a darker side, and it takes more than a beginner's bondage set from Good Vibrations to pound your pulse, you're probably a good candidate for Sociolotron.

Sociolotron is an MMORPG in which you create an avatar to represent you in the game world, a post-apocalyptic London in which anything goes. You can band together with other players and form gangs; you can explore sexual fetishes on your own or with other players; you can become a criminal, a cop, a prostitute, a torturer. In the words of Shawn Rider, reviewer at GamesFirst.com, Sociolotron "is one of those outposts of indy gaming that exists so far outside the mainstream it must be seen as something significantly different."

It's a game where violence and sex come together. Rape is illegal in the game, but not against the game rules. In other words, in-game rapists can be caught and punished by the in-game law enforcement, but the players aren't banned. Sex can result in disease, pregnancy, or other challenges for your character.

Yet sex is an essential part of the game play. You can only produce heirs through sex, and without heirs, you cannot keep all the property you've acquired in the 70 game years allotted to your character's lifespan. (Assuming you survive until the natural end of your life.) Too much sex can reduce your "morality" level; too little and your "satisfaction" level drops. Apparently, neither of these events bode well for your in-game score or survival.

Sociolotron embodies all those things people fear about the internet and sex. It's dark, it's twisted, it gives people permission to do terrible things to themselves and each other. It's a game developed without the resources the big boys like Sony and Electronic Arts command. In that way it embodies a certain internet spirit. Yet it's an environment where you can do those things in perfect safety. You can play underworld criminal while your lover is reading in the next room. You can explore the possibilities of prostitution while outside the game you're slumped in your chair in your oldest sweats, drinking a Diet Coke and eating Cheetos with chopsticks (to avoid coating your keyboard in orange goo).

And yet even this game depends on relationships. Players forge friendships and develop enmities. Through the shared fantasy, people make connections with others who share their particular imaginative tastes.

And the Fur Went Flying

Not all sex-themed games are dark or violent. In a column about in-game cybersex, I inadvertently stirred up trouble when I mentioned a furry-themed BDSM game where players have safe words and great care is taken to make sure all sex play is consensual. So many people clicked through to the site that the game master had to shut down his server until the curious moved on and the serious re-applied for membership.

Furries are people who assume non-human (but sentient) identities for their online role-play: foxes, leopards, centaurs, bears. A few members of the Sex Drive forum are long-time furries, and they are quick to point out that not all furry communities are about sex or kink. You can find "safehouses" for younger furs that permit no sexual behavior at all. After all, the fun part is becoming a non-human and interacting with other non-humans. Any sexual play is just the sprinkles on the donut.

The controversy about my column sparked several threads in the Sex Drive forum about being a furry, furry communities, and why furry players tend to avoid publicity. "Am I a closet furry?" asked more than one person. It got me thinking about what would most appeal to me if I were going to join an online role-playing game. If I had the time, I think I would pick a text-based, furry-themed community.

Back in my Aphrodite days, I had an alternate identity. Not a secret one, but a consistent one. (All I had to do was enter the chat room as Monkey and a regular would shout "look at the knockers on that primate!") Being Monkey let me interact with the others in entirely different ways. I typed all of my interaction as actions or as monkey sounds, no "human talk," and found that I could communicate quite a bit through body language even in chat. I could scamper up to someone's shoulder, make faces, run along the rafters, swing from chandeliers, and generally behave like, well, a sentient if non-verbal monkey. As Monkey, I didn't get propositioned by strangers, and I discovered that while I always tried to maintain a certain dignity as Aphrodite no matter how dirty I was talking, I didn't bother as Monkey.

Oddly enough, a monkey is the last animal I would want to be in a furry community.

I never had any interest in pretending to be a man, or pretending to be someone I wasn't. Aphrodite was always the real me, although not my most Sunday-go-to-meeting me, and so was Monkey. Yet I expressed myself differently under the two handles and would switch names mid-chat if I felt like acting differently.

A game gives structure to a shared fantasy, much more so than a chat room. If you have to pay to join, so much the better, as it weeds out those not serious about the play. And please, do me a favor. If you go Googling or trolling through IRC to check out the furs, please be respectful. They've received a lot of crap from the press and have been portrayed as "perverted sex maniacs." As I learned, they are protective about their communities, as well they should be. Otherwise these worlds would be overrun with trolls and pornbots and idiots whose sole purpose is to cause trouble. Don't storm the castle; knock and wait to be invited in.

Whenever you bring people together in a fantasy setting, sex often becomes part of that fantasy. The difference between chat cybersex and game cybersex is that in the game, you have a structured environment where everyone shares a similar view of the cyber world. If one of you mentions you're in a tree house high above the forest floor and you have to be extra quiet so the Elf King doesn't hear you and get jealous, the other knows what you're talking about. Say something like that in a general cybersex community and you probably won't find the same connection.

One Sex Drive reader says:

> I feel myself thinking about those other
> elves with a grin, and wonder: if I, as a
> person, (and not just my character) have an
> attraction to these other characters (exten-
> sions of real-life people, of course), what
> is going on?!? It seems to be a deeper level
> of identity crisis and confusion than with
> cybersex, wherein the role-playing is super-
> ficial and not a complete identity eclipse.
> The problem has something to do with my
> human emotions getting entangled with my
> character's. What do actors do? You don't
> kiss on stage without feeling something.

In a webcam community like Qnext or PalTalk you see other people in their computer chairs, couches and beds, looking the way they normally look. You might not know

them or even talk to them except during the mutual masturbation session. In a game, you see each other as
avatars, or through text descriptions of the characters
you're playing, and you probably know each other pretty
well by the time you get to cybersex. In-game cyber usually emerges from friendships that grow between players,
and can happen either in or out of character, and sometimes even outside the game. (If the game doesn't have a
way to private message other players, you can always
take the flirting or sex to IM while playing the game in
another window.)

And if sex never happens? At least you have something to do to pass the time.

Simulated Gender

The Sims is a game even non-gamers have heard of. It's a
game that depends upon in-game relationships, although
it is not a multiplayer game. (The Sims Online, which
added a MMORPG component to the game, tanked.) The
first time I played it I was hooked, and I ended up spending weeks playing the game long-distance over the telephone with a friend who lived 400 miles away. He worked
the controls and narrated the action, and we decided
together what to do next. (Who needs phone sex when
you can have phone Sims?)

In The Sims, you are in charge of an individual or a
family of simulated people known as Sims. You make sure
each Sim gets enough food, exercise, recreation and sleep.
You get your Sims to work on time, and you oversee your
Sims' relationships with other Sims. You direct your Sims
with a combination of mouseclicks and key presses and soon
become adept at reading the game's picture-language so
you know when your Sims are hungry, tired or lonely. The

Sims 2 lets you manage entire generations of Sims from birth through death, and sometimes even after death if your Sims come back as ghosts.

When your Sim family is functioning well, your Sims' status meters show high levels of happiness and satisfaction. When you're not helping them take good care of themselves—or when you're indulging in the popular pastime of torturing your Sims—their levels of health and happiness drop.

The goal of the game play is to keep your Sims happy and healthy. But in practice, there's no winning or losing, and if your personal goal is to drive your Sim so bonkers that he dissolves into a quivering lump of jelly who does nothing all day but sit in a corner and shake, you can do that too.

The Sims represents sex—the game calls it "woohoo"—with a comical flurry of animation beneath the blankets. It's nothing pornographic, just a blurring of the covers with the occasional hand or foot peeking out from under the blanket, followed by a sigh.

What you might not expect in a mainstream game marketed to middle America and even casual gamers is the matter-of-fact way in which this mainstream game accepts a spectrum of human sexuality. Sims can be straight or gay, bi or transgendered. Sims of any sex can live together and make woohoo and become parents—through DNA transmission for hetero couples and through adoption for same-sex couples. Gay Sims are not confined to expansion packs and add-ons. They're simply part of the game.

If you're wondering why that's revolutionary, good for you. It did not occur to me that this was anything to write about until I read an article on Gamespot.com in which editor Avery Score did a round-up of U.S.-based games that have homosexual characters. While The Temple of Elemental Evil from Greyhawk Games can reward your male swashbuckler with a gay pirate's hand in marriage and Peter Molyneux's Fable permits multiple spouses of any sex, you have to turn to Japan to find a plethora of games with a wide range of sexual orientations. (Excluding role-playing games, of course, in which you can be whatever gender and orientation you want to be.)

In The Sims 2, interSim relationships are even more important than they were in the first game. Each Sim is given one of five "aspirations"—romance, family, popularity, wealth or knowledge—that they must work toward and achieve in the game. This goal drives some of your options within the game. For example, if your Sim's aspiration is romance, you'll spend more time putting your Sim into social situations. If it's knowledge, your Sim will spend more time reading. And even if your Sim's primary aspiration is wealth, he or she can only get rich through building the right relationships within the game.

The relationship-building is surprisingly complex, considering that these are not avatars representing real human beings but rather animated characters in a game. On my first foray into The Sims 2, I created a hot female Sim with an aspiration for romance, bought her a house in Strangetown, furnished her with a refrigerator and a double bed, and sent her out to lure another woman home.

Unfortunately, I was in a hurry, unwilling to spend the time necessary to let my Sim develop relationships naturally. Within the first two minutes of my Sim's first conversation with a neighboring female Sim (a game character, not one I controlled), I was already right-clicking my Sim to see if my menu of options—the actions I can choose for my Sim to perform, such as "make lunch" or "tell a joke"—included "flirt." After about 10 minutes, the other Sim strode away and would not return. Perhaps she was offended by the way my Sim told all of the male visitors to leave, or perhaps my Sim was too eager.

Or maybe my Sim told one too many jokes. What can I say? I didn't have many actions to choose from. Either way, my Sim was rejected, a common enough event in the real-life relationship game as well. Whether that rejection came from the opposite sex or the same sex makes no difference—it still brought my romance meter down. Romance is romance, regardless of sexual orientation.

The inclusion of gay relationships in The Sims and other games reflects the "Will and Grace" effect American society has been experiencing for the past several years. Yes, half the country is terrified at the thought that somewhere out there a man might be loving another man, but the other half couldn't care less. Fifty years ago, the split would be a lot less even.

When I talked to gamers about gay Sims, most of them either hadn't known it existed or knew but didn't care. Those who did know had experimented with creating gay Sims and managing those relationships. Overwhelmingly, the response I got was "so what?" For the many members of the gamer generation, there's nothing provocative, political or puerile about homosexuality in The Sims—it's simply no big deal. And for the handful of parents who wrote to thank me for writing a column about The Sims 2 so they could now make sure their children are never exposed to the God-forsaken game, all I can say is that I think you're missing the point.

As we continue to redefine human communication and connection through technology, I can imagine a future in which a person's sexual orientation truly makes no difference beyond helping determine who we want to sleep with. Even that depends on a whole set of factors, of which gender is only one. Whether we're gay or straight or somewhere in between will cease to be of concern to

anyone but ourselves and our lovers, and future generations will roll their eyes at their elders and wonder what
all the fuss was about.

Porn Games

Adult games have never been a huge success, probably
because porn and gaming have different purposes. Porn is
something you watch as an adjunct to an external activity
such as masturbation or partner sex, and for most people,
it's something to enjoy in 15-minute increments. Games
are something you set aside time to play, an activity you
try to immerse yourself in deeply enough to retreat from
the outside world for a while. But that hasn't stopped
adult companies from trying to find the perfect fusion of
gameplay and pornography.

I have an interactive DVD that attempts to combine
some elements of game play with porn. It's reminiscent of
the *Choose Your Own Adventure* books of my childhood,
where at critical points in the story you direct whether the
characters will take one action or another. In this adult
game, the ostensible goal is to help Seymore Butts to find
his kidnapped girlfriend Shane, although really the point
is to direct the plot to see as many boobies as possible. You
watch video clips of Seymore in various neighborhoods
and vehicles, and when presented with options about
what direction to turn or whether to get out of the car, you
click the one you think will lead to sex. In my case, it
rarely seemed to, although I did get treated to bosoms
now and then. While a straight man would be more titil-
lated by that than I am—I already have a nice rack that I
can look at any time I want to—I think most men would
have the same response to the game that I did. You can't
get to the porn quickly enough to spark or maintain

arousal, and the game itself is nowhere near absorbing enough to make it fun to play if you're not seeing any sex.

In early 2005, xStream3D's VirtualJenna broke the mold with a sex game starring a computer-generated model of Jenna Jameson (the woman who "put the star in porn star" according to *Rolling Stone*). Even my most hard-core gamer friend had to admit that the graphical quality is about as good as it gets for a mainstream PC game, although he pointed out a few rough spots.

The game has a deceptively simple goal: bring Jenna to orgasm. You have several tools to help you achieve this, ranging from sex toys to male and female sex partners to a disembodied hand. (The developer assures me that this hand will be replaced by something "less gimmicky" in a future release. I must admit that after an initial period of feeling creeped out by the loose body part, I developed an affection for the hand when I started thinking of it as Thing from "The Addams Family.")

You can take the game in a few different directions. You can dress Jenna in a limited selection of outfits (or in nothing at all), pose her for solo or partner sex, or bring her into the virtual studio for an intimate photo shoot.

It's not as easy to "win" as it sounds. Like real women, Jenna's arousal level rises and falls with little apparent connection to what you're doing. I started by stroking her with the hand while stimulating her with a sex toy. Then I tried directing her in several compromising positions with the male character. Despite her repeatedly claiming "I'm almost there," her Excite-O-Meter never climbed all the way to the top.

I suppose that's part of the realism.

And realism is one of the developer's main priorities for VirtualJenna, according to xStream3D president Brad Abram. "Right now we have to back off on the quality of rendering Jenna so it will look good on an 18-month-old PC," said Abram. "But in another year or 18 months, we can crank it up, get more photorealistic, because new PCs have such hot graphics cards (as standard equipment)." In other words, by the time this book hits the shelves, you might have an even more accurate rendition of Jenna to play with.

The graphics quality will still wow casual gamers, although I presume hardcore gamers are accustomed to this level of motion and appearance. Personally, I'm impressed. An extreme close-up of the animated Jenna's naughty bits reveal a striking resemblance to the real-life Jenna's parts, down to the shadow that proves she waxes rather than shaves.

When I tested the game, the play was still basic. But Abram has big plans. "We needed a starting point, and we wanted to get to market," he said. "As we move forward, we are investing the money [we make from subscriptions] into more advanced motion capture and building in the back story and more traditional game challenges."

When you launch VirtualJenna, the game logs onto the internet to download any updates to the models, the toys and other features. This gives players incentive to keep their subscriptions going even after the initial novelty wears off. And the developers understand a fundamental rule of internet culture: the customer is as much a part of the game as the company that makes it. The game will develop based on feedback from subscribers, and the company doesn't waste money developing features no one wants. And so the game evolves in conjunction with the players' vision, not just the developers'.

So what do people want? Based on feedback from an earlier version of the game released in Europe (*sans* Jenna), everything.

"You'd be surprised at how many subscribers tell us they want smells in the game," he says, musing on the possibilities offered by Trisenx's Scent Dome. He also cited development of "a digital Kama Sutra that offers many more options for positioning and pleasuring Jenna."

You'll eventually be able to put yourself into the game using the same "photo personalization technology" used to create the 3-D model of Jenna, and to order customized audio so Jenna can call out your name. Adding real sex toys—for the player, not for Jenna—is another feature on the list.

Abram sees VirtualJenna as the perfect complement to console games, even if Xbox and Playstation developers would not touch content this explicit. "In some games, you can go into a strip club," he said. "Now you can go online (to VirtualJenna) and do whatever you do in the back room, that you can't do in the other games."

But VirtualJenna is not just an adjunct to "real" games, nor is it a novelty that will quickly lose its appeal. It is the foundation for a complex action game that combines elements of James Bond, "The X-Files" and lots and lots of sex. xStream3D plans to deliver this game, tentatively titled Jenna Jameson's Secret Online Service, incrementally each month, so subscribers always have something to look forward to.

I am watching this game carefully. If it develops the way Abram described it in our interview, I can see it or something like it being the break-out title that converges porn and gaming at last. It's a game I might be interested in playing with a partner, in much the same way we might use porn to transition from workaday selves to energetic lovers.

The demand for high-quality adult games definitely exists, despite my gamer buddies' insistence that the two will never mesh well. When I saw the prototype for VirtualJenna at the Adult Entertainment Expo in January 2005, I stood among a crowd that practically vibrated with excitement during the demo. Everyone wanted to try it out. And during a live beta test, when a Norwegian blogger linked to the test site, Abram's server logs showed more than 75,000 unique IDs within hours of the blog post. "We weren't even taking credit card payments yet," he said. "I had to refund 240 people!"

My own reaction to VirtualJenna surprised me more than anything within the game itself. It turns out that my sexual orientation gets in the way of my ability to bring Jenna to climax. I have an aversion to sliding dildos into Jenna's various orifices, and moving the hand over her breasts gives me the willies. Bringing the male character in didn't help much, as you can only touch Jenna; the hand and toys do not work on him.

I was astonished, especially after my attempts to get a lesbian relationship going in The Sims 2. In fact, I once experimented with same-sex cyber when, as Aphrodite, I took a scene with another chat room regular so far that she got uncomfortable and told me by private message to stop. I had no goal or intentions at the time other than to see how far things would go. I realize now it was the cybersex equivalent of chicken, where I was refusing to be the first one to back down.

I've always said that I am 93 percent straight. I couldn't care less who people sleep with or pair off with, and I appreciate female beauty as much as anyone. That I had such a hard time stroking animated breasts is testament to how powerful the fantasy can be.

That's why I think that of all the enhancements planned for VirtualJenna, the fetish room will be the biggest hit. Abram describes it as a place to explore fantasies you would not enact in real life, or that you are too shy or afraid to bring up with a partner. In that sense, it will be like cybersex: a safe place to play that is realistic enough to engage the imagination and convince the mind that you are indeed having the experience.

Being a trouper, I continued with the game despite my hang-ups about participating in girl-on-girl sex. (Sex Drive doesn't write itself!) Pretty soon I wanted to do things that you couldn't do yet, like use the hand to deliver a spanking rather than just a gentle stroke. I wanted to add a cat-o-nine tails to the sex toy library, and I wanted the dildos to vibrate as well as pump. Most of all, I wanted Jenna to have more to say than "oh oh oh" and "I'm almost there."

But despite these limitations, my experience with the game was positive. It was the first sex game I had seen with such a well-rendered environment and beautifully modeled characters. And it's about time we had a game that devotes as much detail and screen time to sex as other games grant to violence.

"The world is ready for something like this," Abram said. "In this game, the women are the stars. They're powerful."

Games on the Go

Mobile content companies have been trying to capitalize on cell phones for years, and have joined the sexual revolution 2.0 with offerings ranging from pornography to sex games for grown-ups. One of the most interesting is not explicit, although it's definitely a game for adults.

Hong Kong-based Artificial Life introduced V-Girl: Your Virtual Girlfriend in late 2004. V-Girl is a game about relationships, and unlike The Sims, it's marketed almost exclusively toward men. It uses technology to simulate a relationship, rather than to simulate sex.

V-Girl is not like The Sims; there are no characters for you to control, and the relationship you're supposed to nurture is between yourself and the AI character, not among the characters themselves. But it does sound like what you might get if you fell in love with one of your Sims.

When you subscribe to V-Girl, an animated character named Vivien comes to (artificial) life on your cell phone screen—as long as you have a 2.75G or 3G mobile phone with Java MIDP 1.0. Vivien can chat, argue and flirt with you through text and audio messages. You can buy her gifts (can you say "product placement"?), take her on virtual dates, and enter her dreams. According to the V-Girl FAQ, the goal of the game is to "make a new friend." Vivien learns about you as the game develops, based on how you interact with her.

I think back to the end of the last century, when an upstart company called Purple Moon began developing computer games for girls. It produced a series of games staring Rockett and her junior high friends, and the company came under fire from critics because part of the game play depended on the girls building relationships with other players and characters. Male game critics had an especially difficult time getting their minds around the game, and their criticism ranged from skeptical to outright vicious.

Despite the devotion of the girls who loved the adventures—and who generated 12 million page views a month at the Rockett website—the critics turned out to be right about one thing: this type of game, at that time, was not profitable. And Purple Moon did eventually go out of business.

Now, only a few years later, we have a female AI character starring in a "relationship" game marketed toward men. The difference is that this game contains adult subject matter—no, not sex, but Vivien is 21 and can go to bars—and it doesn't require players to sit at a computer or blatantly engage in gameplay. You can dip into the game whenever you have a few moments, and because it's not X-rated, you can do it while standing in line at the bank or waiting for your flight in a crowded airport.

Robert, a Sex Driver reader, pointed out a side benefit of the game that I hadn't thought of. "Vivienne might give us guys some practice in how to converse and be civil," he says. "The mother-in-law bit I can do without, though. I used to have one."

When you can flirt over SMS with real people, can Vivien the V-Girl compete? It's hard to predict whether V-Girl will succeed. When V-Boy is on the market, when other companies come out with competing games, when a greater variety of characters are available, that's when we'll find out whether we're interested enough in pretend relationships to pay for them.

Why Games Matter

Games are a social activity. You can invite people over for a game party; you can sit in your slob clothes and social-ize online, in and out of a game, with other players. A game gives us a playground where our imaginations can roam almost as freely as they did when we were children. A game like Second Life in which you build gravity-defying buildings, make crazy outfits for characters to wear, and fly instead of walk invites you to exercise your imagina-tion and ingenuity. And yes, cybersex sometimes emerges between Lifers.

Life inside the games is similar to real life, except the normal rules don't apply. You can let aspects of yourself roam free that you might not be comfortable with exposing in your offline life. That's one reason violence is still more prevalent than sex in American video games. Most gamers can experience sex for real, but they aren't going to get to blast a thousand monsters out of the city with a machine gun on a regular basis.

If you want to experiment with gender, sexual orientation, species, a game gives you a goal to work toward, puzzles to solve, and a safe environment in which other players will accept you for the sentient creature you are. A real-life introvert can be the life of the party at an in-game tavern, while the real-life class clown might indulge a serious or introspective streak in the fantasy world. Because you have something to do other than sex, you don't get all hung up on whether the other person is really male or female, young or old, human or Elf. You can accept them as they present themselves and get on with surviving, or questing, or whatever it is your particular game calls for.

And that's a lesson we could all stand to learn in our lives outside the game.

Talking About the Revolution

Come to www.reginalynn.com to discuss gaming in the Sex Drive forum.

> *Has your game play ever become romantic or sexual?*
> *Have you experimented with gender roles in games?*
> *What do you think about the convergence of porn and games?*

REVOLUTIONARY PROFILE
Patric Lagny

Patric Lagny is the mastermind behind Sociolotron, an independent, adults-only online role-playing game. Sociolotron is a game in which players can do just about anything as long as they do it in character and in the game. It has come under scrutiny for allowing players to explore the darker sides of their natures, and it is a game environment no big development company was willing to touch—thus prompting Patric to build it himself.

How many players do you have for the beta version of Sociolotron?

At peak times, we have 150 or 160 people logged in at the same time. But the total active player base is hard to determine. In the past two years we had about 9,000 people sign up. Not all of them stayed, probably because we're in development. We'll be out of beta later this year though—we're just doing the rest of the bug fixes now.

Overt sexual behavior in an online role-playing game? What were you thinking?

People want to have, and do have, cybersex all the time in role-playing games. That's been the thing ever since the beginning of electronic communication. I saw it on Compuserve in '86. When I started to play Ultimate Online back in '97 or '98, I met a girl—supposedly—who was hooking around. She put up ads on billboards in the game. But she very quickly got into trouble. The game masters popped up, and she said "I'm just role playing," but afterwards she had to hide her activities.

That gave me the impression that somebody should do something where you CAN be sexual.

Is anyone else developing anything like this?

This is my own theory. I started doing game development in 1993, and every company I've worked for has talked about sex games. With all those horny toads, all those geeks, sex games are a natural discussion topic. People were thinking or saying, somebody should do it, why don't we do it? We can't do it because have a reputation.

Whenever I was at a company that was financially desperate, they'd talk about doing sex games. Then when the next round of financing came around, sex games were already forgotten. The programmers said the same thing—somebody should do it, just not me, what about my reputation.

Maybe it comes from the fact that the first sex games on the market were only these strip poker things, jigsaw puzzles, flash animation. People who do that got reputations for being low-level programmers who could just do Macromedia things. So nobody wants to get into it and get that type of reputation and then be out of the games field.

Did you not worry about your reputation?

I'm kind of out of the big business already. I moved to Los Angeles in 2001 and tried to find a job here in the game industry, but it was hard. I'm mostly too old for it, they want youngsters they can exploit for no wages. So I guess at 43 I'm too old for it anyway and don't need to worry so much about my reputation.

Does Sociolotron change people's lives?

I am always hearing from people who say they met their boyfriend or girlfriend through the game. I even heard from one couple who moved to a different city so they could be together. (They wrote to me to say thank you!)

Otherwise, not much, except for the time they spend playing. I hear from people who spend every free minute here, but that's not a big deal, not special to us—any game has people who spend more time there than the average player. It's just a game where you can act out certain fantasies that you can't do elsewhere. And you can find like-minded people. We don't discriminate against people's fantasies. We're trying to be quite open and give everyone a place. But I don't think we're changing their lives to a great extent.

When I type in Sociolotron in Google, I find a lot of websites that talk about it. It's mostly negative, with a focus on the rape stuff, when that's really just a small part of the entire game. I hope Sociolotron can be part of the movement that helps people to free themselves a little bit more, to express themselves in the way they want to without those restrictions you have with our conservative government and the crusade against porn and what people do in their bedrooms.

Why is everyone so afraid of a game like Sociolotron?

Speaking from my personal opinion, it's not really fear, it's political correctness. Everyone is afraid to do everything. They're afraid to light a cigarette at the beach [in California] because the police might come at them. It's the same with this. There's a game out there now where your character can rape another character, and even though that's just one little feature of the game, it's a big deal for people. Now come all the websites saying that they're against this. They never point out you can also rape male characters in the game, or anything else that happens when you're playing. It's just political correctness, because if they write something positive, someone might confront them about the negative. And it's sensationalism too, to bring people in. It's better to write "this game allows rape" than "this game lets you do cybersex."

7

Blogs and Online Diaries: Publishing Your Privates

The web has done a fine job of coaxing out the voyeur and the exhibitionist in all of us. It practically begs you to post pictures of your dog and kids, to comment on various products and services, and to read other people's diaries, while letting them read yours. Pew Research reported in 2004 that more than 53 million American adults had used the internet to publish their thoughts, respond to others, post pictures, share files, and otherwise contribute to the explosion of content available online.

News agencies worry about blogs. Journalists worry about bloggers. Politicians worry about staffers who blow and tell (although apparently not enough to stop sleeping with them). Even employers worry about blogs. The social networking site Friendster, which encourages blogging among its members, fired engineer Joyce Park for mentioning the company in her blog—even though her posts were considered innocuous, and even more Friendster-friendly than not, by everyone else.

Blogs and online diaries are not exactly the same thing, although the terms have come to be synonymous. I tend to use the term "blogger" to describe anyone who keeps a blog or an online diary, and "blog" to refer to blogs, journals and diaries. But just to be clear:

A blog, or "web log," started as a way to link to and comment on other web pages in a logbook format. A blog isn't necessarily personal, and in fact, it often isn't. My own blog was a list of books I've read, with commentary and the occasional song lyric or movie review. (I had to stop blogging when my workload became overwhelming, but I hope to get back to it someday.) Slashdot.org is a public blog that disseminates "news for nerds." Boing Boing.net is "a directory of wonderful things."

An online diary is just that, a personal space where diarists write about their lives, sometimes in excruciating detail. Some diary authors keep their journals strictly private, while others restrict access to readers they have authorized. And some put their deepest thoughts and personal desires out there for everyone to see, regardless of whether it scares the horses.

When else in history have so many people combined literacy with easy and cheap access to a publishing medium—a medium that reaches across political borders, time zones and computing platforms as if such obstacles barely exist? And when else in history were so many people writing about their sex lives in such detail, in public?

When Sex Drive goes live each week, I email the URL to my friends so they can read it. (And I know you all eagerly await this announcement each week. Go on, admit it.) More than one person has asked me if I know how revealing these columns are. (Yup.) They wonder if baring my thoughts on sex and technology causes me trouble in my day job as a freelance technical writer. (Not so far.) They ask me if I worry about my other clients "finding out" (sometimes) or about being stalked (BTDT, won't let it happen again).

The thing is, when you spend enough time exploring sexuality and technology—whether in the guise of Aphrodite, chat room diva or Regina Lynn, sex-tech columnist—you get desensitized to what is "appropriate" to share. The line between public and private becomes blurred to the point where the private *is* public. I have always been open about talking about sex. Writing about it (and having it!) on a regular basis keeps it on my mind enough that I tend to ramble on when the topic comes up in conversation.

When I was the only one in my circle whose appropriateness filter was failing, I spent a lot of drives home cringing over what I'd said at the party/networking event/baby shower I'd just attended. But now, I'm no longer alone. One of the most culture-changing aspects of the sexual revolution 2.0 (for Americans, anyway) is this newfound ability to *talk* about sex. In fact, now we can't stop talking about it. It's on TV, in advertising, in the news, on the radio—and not just in the commercials. I suspect that women have always talked about sex when they get together, but now it's talked about in mixed groups.

Part of this comes from mass media's continuing push to be more shocking, more titillating or more attention-grabbing—and its attempt to compete with the internet. Content providers who want to do what they please without the Federal Communications Commission breathing down their necks for every swear word or bare breast have finally gotten what they've needed to become self-sustaining: mass adoption of broadband connections. Internet radio has been a viable option for listeners for years; now internet TV and movies have a chance to shine.

Publishing by and for the People

Mass media versus the internet is not the whole story, though. Individuals all over the world are seizing their chance to say those things on the internet that might be outrageous, offensive, illegal or downright dangerous to say anywhere else.

Through technology, anyone can publish their memoirs, uncensored and unedited, and therefore, anyone does. We all have a shot at becoming the next Samuel Pepys, the next Anaïs Nin, without having to know someone in publishing or becoming professional writers. The sheer number of blogs and online diaries proves that people everywhere are willing—even eager—to publish their most secret thoughts where anyone in the world can read them. And the popularity of such blogs proves that people everywhere are willing to read them.

Like sex, these technologies help us establish a one-on-one connection with another human being. The intimacies revealed in a public journal might resonate with the private fears of a reader in such a way that the reader discovers she is not alone, not an anomaly, not a freak. No matter how many readers (or lovers) you have, this soul-bearing form of communication is so personal that you simply cannot connect in the same way with a crowd. Of course there's an element of exhibitionism to the broadcast of clandestine contemplation. But there's also a reaching out, a questing for communion and empathy, a vulnerable "this is me at my most naked." For both the writer and the reader, it is the culmination of a search to find acceptance in at least one other person's heart.

In a culture where sex sells everything from cigarettes to panty liners, where else are we to go for the sense of mystery if not our innermost thoughts, written as if in the confessional but shared with all?

When the Private Goes Public

I love the whole concept of blogging. It's one of my favorite aspects of the web. I love how each author becomes a celebrity in a small circle, and the roles of writer and reader become fluid as everyone in the community is both writer and reader. But I am not blind to blogs' destructive potential when it comes to our sex lives.

Sometimes the best way to keep a relationship healthy is to keep your secrets secret. Because when the private goes public, you aren't the only one who is exposed.

Blogging everything can hinder a developing romance or break up a relationship. Even if you attempt to disguise identities by using initials or code words, people recognize themselves, or suspect they know who you're writing about. Jessica Cutler, the Washington, D.C. staffer who got fired for blogging about the sex she was having with several married co-workers, may have ended up infamous and in possession of a lucrative book deal, but that's only because she was first. And not everyone is in as high-profile of a position as she was, and not everyone is identifying elected officials in their blogs. In other words, you might end up dateless, jobless and humiliated, without a book deal to comfort you in your distress.

Do we really need to be privy to every nuance of our partners' insecurities and worries about the relationship? Thoughts are only fleeting when they aren't published. When you blog, you record your impressions of the moment. Even if you've been thinking about a topic for a long time, if you continue to think about it after you blog it, you're likely going to find a new perspective or even reverse your opinion altogether. That happened to me occasionally with my book blog, where I would rave or rant about a book and then two months later write another post explaining my current thinking about that book. I don't go back and delete or edit older posts; I assume readers will keep the temporal nature of blogging in mind when they comb through my archives.

The fact is, those original thoughts—that is, your thought of that moment, on that day, in that mood, under those circumstances—may be permanently ascribed to you as your unchanging opinion for the rest of your life. If you post when you're hurt or angry and your beloved reads it, he or she might assume you feel that way all the time. You think you're just venting, and in fact, the act of writing it all out has therapeutic benefits. You blog and feel better.

Then the people you've blogged about read the post and feel like you have punched them in the face. They wonder why you're blaming them for this, or suspect you're lying about that, and throughout runs the question: who gave you the right to publish anything at all about them? And meanwhile you barely remember what you were upset about now that you've let go of it through writing.

It's easy to get carried away when you blog. No editor looks over your work. Nobody acts as a filter for what you should or shouldn't say. That's one reason blogs are so popular, but it's also a reason they can be anathema to a relationship. And if you go too far, there's no taking it back. Google might have already cached the page. Reblogging later to say that "back then I thought A, but now I know B," is only effective when the reader catches the more recent post.

The main difference between the leather-bound journal I keep near my bed and my blog is that the blog has a potential readership of millions. My journal has a readership of one (me). I can go months without writing in my journal and nobody notices. Yet when I ran out of time to blog, I posted a notice that the blog was on hiatus. Wouldn't want to disappoint any of my five readers!

I'm starting to hear stories from couples who struggle with how one partner's blog intrudes on their private time. The external audience, whether real or imagined, creates pressure on a blogger to update, to post at least every couple of days, even when on a romantic retreat or a week-long cruise. A partner may not be so patient and understanding when she finds you in the bathroom at 3 a.m., hunched over your laptop, banging out descriptions of the places you explored that day—on your honeymoon.

How Blogs Can Help a Relationship

For someone who is willing to reveal just about anything in pursuit of a good column, I'm coy when it comes to blogging. I save personal relationship challenges for my private journal. These may end up in a column later on when I've thought them through, if they're relevant to that week's topic, but I'm certainly not exposing my raw, meandering thoughts as they happen.

Yet I know some people who vow, specifically, to journal everything online regardless of the consequences. One woman committed to one year of "public therapy" in an online diary. No, she didn't have online chats with counselors. Rather, she chronicled her recovery from a debilitating depression that involved a stay in the hospital. Her friends, including her ex-boyfriend and her current boyfriend, were permitted and even encouraged to read this diary (especially the ex-boyfriend, who deserved it), and yet she lived in fear that her employer would find out. Considering the number of times she mentioned sex, drugs and rock'n'roll, she had reason to be nervous.

When the year had passed, she found she had rebuilt her self and her life so completely, she no longer had need for the public diary. She cancelled her account and pulled the entire thing offline, and that was that. She has no archive, no file that records all those posts. Journaling is process, not product; you don't need to save it to save yourself.

Another woman, Diane, used to torture herself by reading her ex-boyfriend's diary. He chronicled his affair—the one that led to his jilting her—and recorded his attempts to "be friends" with her after they broke up. His entries were not only unkind, they were occasionally untrue. Diane worried that their circle of mutual friends, all of whom had access to both his diary and hers, and who kept diaries of their own, were going to judge her based on his posts. For a while it became a knot too tangled to untie as various people began to point-counterpoint the diaries.

But as the diaries revealed more and more about personalities and perspectives, my friend began to see that the relationship had been a bad match from the beginning. She learned who her true friends were through the way they responded to both diaries, whether they asked questions and voiced reality checks rather than simply accepted without thinking everything she or her ex wrote. When she was ready, one of those true friends began to court her, and now a few years later they are ecstatic in love and marriage and planning a baby.

It's easy to step back and say, "Well, duh, if it hurts, don't read it." I've always felt that if you read someone's journal or personal communication, you deserve whatever you find. Yet a public blog isn't exactly hidden under the mattress. Sometimes it's just too hard to ignore, especially if your friends start asking you about it.

Some people find that despite the pain a partner's diary can cause, reading it is worth the risk for the insight it provides. My friend Kay reads and comments in her boyfriend's journal almost daily, even when neither of them are traveling. Before they moved in together, before they were "exclusive," there was a tense week when he became fascinated with a waitress who chatted him up over the weekend. Being an honest, communicative man, he told Kay about it. Her response? "I don't want to hear about it," even though at the time he was free to do whatever he felt was right. That didn't stop her from reading his online journal, though, and she had to coach herself through it while he wrestled with his feelings for her and for the other woman. She knew better than to say "figure it out yourself" and then complain to him or get angry about his doing just that, but that didn't make it easy to read it all in real-time.

It worked out in her favor, but it took a lot of conscious effort on Kay's part to get through it, especially when she knew she had the option not to read the blog. She confesses now that dipping periodically into the diaries of his two most recent ex-girlfriends has given her some insight into his patterns, and some of his past, which has helped her be more patient with his idiosyncrasies. They now have one of the most intimate, passionate relationships of anyone I know.

Why Blogs Matter

You can see why blogs pose challenges to lovers that no previous technologies could. An etiquette is emerging in the blogging community that may reinforce the creed of "honor among bloggers." It includes the obvious guidelines, like don't identify your friends (even by their initials) without their permission and don't blog about your employer if you cannot afford to lose your job.

I'd like to see a Blogging Code arise in which no matter how much you wish to avenge yourself on a faithless girlfriend, a one-night stand gone bad, or a spouse who preferred the Pandora Peaks CybOrgasMatrix to you, you still do not expose them in your blog. From what I've seen, the blogger gets into as much trouble as the blogged, and online revenge tends to reflect more poorly on the avenger than the avengee.

As we become accustomed to getting inside each other's heads through blogs, we may end up adapting how we interact with one another. I hope we don't become guarded, afraid to say anything revealing because it might end up blogged. Part of the Blogging Code will have to be an agreement not to blog anything the other person asks to be off the record. Like journalists, bloggers need to respect their sources, or their sources will stop feeding them information.

Blog posts, like email, are monologues. When lovers read each other's musings it gives another insight to what's going on inside the other person's mind. We blog differently than we talk, and the way we connect our thoughts to world events through linking and commenting certainly reveals a side of us our partner might not otherwise see. Like email, a blog post can open up a subject for discussion. Unlike email, a blog opens up that subject to every netizen who surfs through. Input from strangers may be just the thing to make you admit you're being stubborn, pathetic, dramatic or controlling. Comments from others who have been in your shoes might be the difference between an impulse reaction and a considered decision.

A blog can become a public record of your current and past relationships. If that's not what you want, you might choose to keep your love life out of your public diary. It'll be interesting to watch blogs and blogging over the next 10 years and see how much of our relationships wind up on the public internet.

Rebecca Blood, author of *We've Got Blog: How Weblogs Are Changing Our Culture*, has no qualms about which way she prefers. "I never post anything personal in my blog," she says.

Talking About the Revolution

Come to www.reginalynn.com to discuss blogs in the forums.

Have you become more or less public about your private life since the internet?

Has your blog gotten you into trouble?

Do you think people should blog their relationships?

REVOLUTIONARY PROFILE
Adam Penenberg

Adam L. Penenberg is an assistant professor at New York University and the assistant director of the business and economic reporting program in the department of journalism. He writes the weekly Media Hack column at Wired News.

You said when you wrote about blogger Mary Hodder, a woman who spends most of her life online, you got a big response from readers. What triggered that flood of email?

I didn't mean that column to be flattering or critical. It was just about how she lives her life digitally. To Mary, online relationships can be more real in some ways than face-to-face relationships.

That's because she's online all the time, and she'll come across an idea or a meme or an article she likes, and immediately blog it. Then her friends, associates, colleagues, whoever else reads her blog and responds by email, IM or cell phone to talk about it. She'll have this running conversation with her virtual relationships at the same time she is interacting with reality.

Are blogs transforming our culture?

Bloggers have relationships with each other. What is cross-linking but a relationship? They mention each other all the time, they share traffic. And blogging sets up a whole conversation that anyone can join in. Those relationships can become more real than real relationships—and help you find community of like-minded geeks.

Blogging certainly acts as a huge quality control program for the press. It used to be that we journalists would write a story or a column and we might receive three letters in the mail. You never really knew what the impact of a story was, or even if anyone actually read it. When they did read it, you didn't know what they were doing with it.

Now, my column goes live and in minutes someone is blogging on it, giving their reaction. Sometimes what they say is not well thought out. But a lot of times it is, and they know more about a subject than I do, or they point out something I could have developed more. And that's really instructive.

I write, someone reacts, someone reacts to their reactions, someone else brings in more material, and an incredible discussion will spread.

Every column now is a process, not just the research and writing of it, but the aftermath. I keep learning. I like that a lot, and if I do make a mistake I hear about it immediately. This is a wonderful thing.

What can a blog tell you about a person?

I've always looked at the internet like one grand Victorian ball. I say that because in these Victorian balls, people would wear costumes and tolerate the most outrageous behavior as long as you were wearing a mask. Those were very repressive times, but you get a little liquor in people and whatever else, and they would act outrageously. Even though people kind of knew who it was, they didn't really know.

The internet is like that. It brings out the most primal behavior in people. And even though digital technology is kind of alienating, it also brings us closer to who we really are. I think this is fascinating.

8

Living Together: How Tech Brings Us Closer

Cars, home appliances and the internet have made it possible to build a life without relying on a partner just to survive. Women can support themselves financially and men can do their own laundry. Most of us aren't in the position of having to marry into a particular family to form appropriate political or financial alliances. It has even become more socially acceptable to be an unmarried parent. And with the divorce rate as high as it is, why would anyone bother to marry at all?

That's like saying that because we have online porn, teledildonics and role-playing games, we no longer need to bother with offline relationships.

Humans are social. We need to bond with one another, we need touch and we need sex. The fundamentalist Christian idea of procreative monogamy may not be everybody's ideal, but if you ask around, most people do expect to pair up with somebody else. Or several some-bodies, in a series or all at once.

What has changed are some of the reasons why we get married or commit to a lifetime partner. We're in an uncomfortable place right now, caught between the traditional relationship roles and the ways we're expanding those roles.

I've discovered through my column and my conversations that my perspective on the single/couple question is somewhat atypical, as I went about my life backwards. I fell in love with a boy in high school, dated him through college, moved in with him the afternoon of my last final exam and married him within the year. I had doubts about getting married but never voiced them to anyone. Marriage was what you did after college, and he was a great partner and an amazing man. I felt like I must be crazy to feel so empty, so doubtful, to be looking at us thinking "is this it?" For the first half of my 20s, I had a perfect life with a good job, a beautiful San Francisco apartment and a man who adored me. How ungrateful of me to wish I were alone!

When I moved out of our apartment—and out of San Francisco—we had been together for 12 years. We had supported each other through lean times, and took pride in one another as we accomplished various career and creative milestones. To this day we agree that we showed each other our potential, and we laid the foundation for the successes we have found in our personal lives and our careers.

If I had realized earlier that we didn't have to follow the old rules about marriage, would we still be married today? I'm not sure. What I do know is that living solo suits me better than living together. That is not the case for everyone. I'm just glad that I have the choice.

Living Solo

Single people are buying cars and houses on our own. We're taking ourselves to dinner and the movies, hanging out with friends or "tribes" instead of dating individuals, building close friendships with people of all genders. We can hire people to handle tasks that would be on a "honey-do list" in a traditional marriage. I have a house-keeper—a gay man—who comes every other Thursday and does a better job in six hours than I could do in six days. (He also brings me houseplants and keeps them alive. This is a domestic miracle.) Cybersex and online dating make it easy to find sexual partners. Take-out and microwaves eliminate the need to learn how to cook; urban folks can even pay for wash-n-fold laundry service if they like.

In other words, a modern professional can pretty much fulfill all of life's basic needs without having to get married. And yet, we do. Why?

Because for most people, committing to a partner and having children is the paramount part of our lives. It doesn't matter how many technical whizzbangs we come up with, we still want to raise a family of our own. The cool thing is that with technology removing some of the "have to" reasons to marry, we can move right on to the "want to" reasons.

Obviously this is a trend that started long before the sexual revolution 2.0, but it's only since the advent of the internet that we have had the flexibility in our jobs to support the choices we make in our relationships. How many of you telecommute sometimes? How many of you run your own businesses from home? How many stay-at-home parents manage to connect, socially and professionally, in ways that would have been impossible just 10 years ago? And how many of you work with people whose success in negotiating flexible schedules inspires other employees to do the same?

The sheer numbers of women and men coming out as "quirkyalones"—who in past ages might have been accused of witchcraft, homosexuality or insanity—signal the massive changes to come in our expectations about living solo and living together.

In her book *Quirkyalone: A Manifesto for Uncompromising Romantics*, author Sasha Cagen describes how she coined the term "quirkyalone" to describe a lifestyle made possible by revolutions in sex and technology. A quirkyalone is a person who enjoys being single and who doesn't date just for the sake of being part of a couple. The instant I came across the word, I knew I had found a label that would help me explain myself to my mom. And apparently thousands of other single men and women felt the same, because Cagen has been inundated with letters and emails from readers all over the world thanking her for helping them feel (ironically) less alone.

These folks aren't opposed to relationships—in fact, they are committed romantics who lean toward idealism and prefer to remain single, for their entire life if necessary, rather than settle for less-than. But even if quirkyalones fall in love (and become quirkytogethers), the relationship does not consume them, and they lead independent, fulfilling lives as individuals as well as a couple.

Cagen's writings about quirkyalones in the late 1990s struck a chord among the many 20- and 30-somethings who thought they were the only ones who enjoyed being single. In an essay published in the Utne Reader in October 2000, Cagen explains:

> We are the puzzle pieces who seldom
> fit with other puzzle pieces. Romantics,
> idealists, eccentrics, we inhabit single-dom
> as our natural resting state. In a world
> where proms and marriage define the social

order, we are, by force of our personalities
and inner strength, rebels.

Technology has made it possible for us to realize
many of the ideals put forth in the first sexual revolution.
Today's professionals may take for granted their ability to
go it alone, but it wasn't that long ago that such an
arrangement was not only socially awkward, it was practically impossible.

I have a friend who met her husband during her first
year of law school. They lived about an hour and a half
apart, too far to drive for weekday overnights but close
enough to spend weekends together. They married during her second year even though they were not going to
be able to move in together until she graduated. Even during school breaks, they typically had to live apart due to
work and volunteer obligations in their respective towns.
But eventually, the day came, and they sold her house.

Within a year, they decided to live separately again.
"We are just a lot happier when we don't live together full
time," she says. "We talk every night for an hour, and
we'll see each other two or three nights a week. It's truly
better this way."

They are not the only married couple to step outside
the traditional arrangement to make the situation work
better for them. Three times in the past year, *O: The Oprah
Magazine* has published articles about married couples
who choose to live apart on a full- or part-time basis. One
couple spends a semester a year in different cities while
the husband teaches at a different university. Another has
two apartments in the same city and spends most of their
nights together at one or the other.

Thanks to IM, the Sinulator, email and cell phones, a
long-distance relationship is not insurmountably difficult

to maintain. For people like me who are in a wonderful relationship they don't want to give up, and yet who prefer to live alone, it's nice to know that those things are no longer mutually exclusive. And for married couples who might otherwise have had only two choices, stay together or break up, technology offers a foundation on which to build whatever kind of alternative arrangement suits them.

All Together Now

One of the consequences of sex is children. And one of the consequences of children can be the lack of sex. Sex may be on our minds but it's not getting through to our bodies.

While we'd all like to have time for lots of foreplay in a romantic setting, the reality is that couples tend to fall into bed two hours later than they wanted to, wrung out from the day's demands. Parents who stay home with small children all day often find that their lives are defined by poop. Feed the baby, change the diaper, feed the baby, change the diaper. On top of that is the schedule of preschool, doctor's appointments, grocery shopping (with the kids!), laundry, housework and the other activities that go into making a home. And for many, it's not just about babies. Children and pets go together, which means it's not just diapers. Feed the dog, pick up the dog poop, feed the dog, pick up the dog poop.

One Sex Drive reader told me:

> I scientifically determined that we have a poop-to-sex ratio of 21 to 1. Two dogs at two times a day each. Two children at two times a day each. Two adults at one time a day. That's nine times a day, or sixty-three times a week. We have sex an average of three times per week.

After that, how anyone could expect you to feel sexy on a moment's notice is beyond me.

Those of us who spend our days at an office or other workplace often underestimate the completely un-sexy day our partners are having at home. We start to think the at-home parent is lounging around, relaxing, watching TV, making interesting meals, playing with happy kids, and generally having a great time. Meanwhile we're in and out of meetings, struggling to keep up with changing priorities and deadlines, working on group projects, doing things on our computers and coping with idiot drivers during our rush-hour commutes. We wonder why our partners are tired, frazzled or cranky when we walk through the door in the evening. After all, aren't we the ones who just had a hard day at work?

Both perspectives are legitimate. Jobs are stressful, parenting is stressful, and whether you do one or both it takes a toll on your libido. By the time everyone is fed, bathed and tucked in, it's not surprising that couples collapse in bed exhausted. Yet if you don't renew your connection to each other, if you don't work to sustain the passion, your relationship is in danger of fizzling out. You'll become automatons who take care of everyone's needs, both at the office and the home front, but who don't nurture your own relationship. When that happens, a fling—whether at the office or in cyberspace—is going to sound awfully tempting.

Technology can make it easier to have a sex life while your children are young. If you're not the type to rent or buy "couples movies" or just don't want to risk your child discovering the DVDs, you have the entire internet at your fingertips. Pornography that turns you both on is one way to jump-start the libido after a long day. This doesn't mean you're not attracted to each other, that you've become inadequate, or that your relationship sucks because it now depends on a crutch. It means that you recognize sex as an important part of your life together, and you will use all of the tools at your disposal to make sure you hang on to it. Frankly, it's too much to ask that you are always in the mood at the same time.

We have the obligation to each other, to our relationships, to our families to keep the intimacy alive. Enjoying sexual imagery together is a far cry from having one partner develop an obsession with internet porn, and it is a way to transition from the stress of the day into the comfort of each other.

One Sex Drive reader emailed me her story about how she overcame her aversion to pornography. "I realized it wasn't about who was more beautiful or more exciting or more anything than me. It was just about sex. So what?" She continued:

> We began incorporating porn into our sexual repertoire when our child was about two. For me, the porn is a distraction from the day-to-day demands of keeping house and raising a child. It's hard to think about diapers when watching Jenna Jameson and her husband sharing intimacy on a massage table. Even better, the movies provide my brain with a fantasy or a setting to imagine my husband and me in, like a tropical island or a pizza parlor (LOL). For my husband, it's very simple: Sex on TV. Cool. It makes him want to have sex with me.

If you truly can't stand the idea of porn in the bedroom (or wherever), you have other options. Sounds Erotic.com produces erotic audio tracks in which women read stories ranging from the romantic to the steamy to the explicit. (The founders hire female readers so male listeners don't feel like there's another man in the room.) You can buy the albums on CD or download them from Audible.com. The husband and wife team who founded the company did so as a way to help couples transition from day job to love life in a natural, non-intrusive way—and quickly enough to do something about it before someone falls asleep.

If your children can read, you probably don't keep erotic books lying around. (I don't care how well you think they're hidden, your kids will find them.) Sex Drive readers have good things to say about CleanSheets.com and Literotica.com, two online magazines devoted to erotic stories. Reading these to each other, or composing a story together to submit to the sites, definitely shifts the brain from work mode to sex mode.

Just one caveat: Learn how to clear your browser cache if you absolutely cannot afford separate computers for yourself and your kids. No point in leaving those naughty URLs in your internet history.

Sex toys can help too, especially for a woman who may have a harder time getting aroused if she's feeling uncomfortable in her post-baby body. Previously sensitive areas might feel less so; previously unresponsive areas might have become sensitive to the lightest touch. Did you know you can use a Hitachi Magic Wand as part of a neck and shoulder massage? Kinky, but true. Or slip on a fingertip vibrator , which feels good for both partners and is quiet enough that you are not going to have little ones knocking on the door asking what you're building in there.

I remember one night in 1974 when I was small, lying abed trying to place a sound I was hearing. I finally decided it must be the blender. I got all excited, and I climbed out of bed, padded out to the living room, and announced "I know, eggnog!" (My parents used to make "eggnog" in the blender using one egg, nonfat milk, a dash of sugar and a teaspoon of vanilla. This was before anyone got paranoid about salmonella. And it's delicious—I still make it.)

Luckily for my parents, they were hanging curtain rods. The sound I'd heard was a power drill, not the blender. But now, having tested many a vibrator for research purposes, I realize the disaster that could have befallen had the sound been coming from the bedroom instead.

Smooth Operations

My sister Patricia and her husband have been married for more than 10 years—just long enough to remember a relatively tech-free relationship. He's a techie who works at an office, she's a musician who stays home with the kids. When I asked her whether technology made a difference in their lives, her face lit up. She rattled off several ways in which cell phones, an SMS-enabled pager and email make their marriage smoother today than it was 10 years ago.

"Marriages take more work than other relationships, especially when you have kids, because it's more important that a person doesn't get bored and leave," she says. "Having ways to make togetherness more convenient is a good thing." She emailed me a list of the most common ways in which technology enhances their relationship. They may sound like little things, but as we all know, it's the aggregation of little things that make or break a relationship.

Here are her suggestions:

Coordinating errands. Being able to communicate any time, any place, makes errands much more efficient.

Whoever is shopping can call home to verify what type of milk to buy or what video to rent. It saves on duplicate trips and gas money, but the main benefit is having more time together at the end of the day.

Love notes. They send quick notes to each other throughout the day.

Accountability. People don't like to admit it, she says, but having such access to one another provides an undeniable benefit to the relationship. You know your husband's not sneaking around on you when he always answers his phone or pager. When your wife's emails always originate from a predictable location like home or office, you know she's where she says she is. More communication and connection means more trust, Patricia says.

Attention. One fundamental part of a relationship is to pay attention to one another. The caller gets to have contact whenever he wants it; the callee knows she is wanted and needed.

Communication. "Duh," she says. One basic example is that you can tell each other things as you think of them, rather than trying to remember at the end of the day. You don't feel like you're living totally separate lives with nothing in common to talk about in the evenings, because you were right there with each other the whole time.

Family involvement. You can text each other immediately with important news—like "I'm not pregnant!" or "the kid has an ear infection"—without having a personal conversation where your coworkers can overhear it.

Safety. Whether out jogging, or running out of gas, or letting a technician from the power company into the backyard, she feels safer when she can contact her husband any time, from any place. "If I end up missing, there's a trail," she says, laughing. "Or he can be my dreamy rescuer—and that's sexy!"

Even if you aren't married and don't have kids, couples who live together can take advantage of the internet to keep the relationship interesting. One of my friends sent me a list of everything she had done online in the past six months. Well, maybe not everything, but everything she was going to share for this book:

- Order flowers and gifts for him
- Make dinner reservations
- Buy movie tickets online
- Order dinner from restaurants that deliver
- Find out what's going on around town
- Buy sex toys and lube
- Buy sexy or slutty costumes
- Reserve a wine-tasting tour
- Buy plane tickets for our next vacation
- Make car rental reservations
- Order gourmet meals
- Make massage reservations
- Reserve a room in a motel with a jacuzzi for a romantic weekend
- Get wine and chocolates delivered to the room by sending an email ahead of our arrival

At the end of her list, she gave an example of how she had used the internet just that morning to plan a surprise for her boyfriend. "I used the [alternative weekly paper's website] to discover that the local adult cinema was having a Couples Free night tonight. I reserved us tickets to see *Bangcock Sluts*. HAHAHA. I even looked up the movie on the Internet Adult Film Database (www.iafd.com) to see what it was about!"

Why Living Together Matters

I read somewhere that the baby boom ended the night Johnny Carson went on the air.

If late-night TV truly renews the bonds between you each night, by all means, have at it. But take advantage of TiVo (or, if you must, an old-fashioned VCR) and watch your shows together when you're less tired.

We have the obligation to our partners to keep the intimacy alive. For most, sex is an integral part of that intimacy. Is it any wonder that so many of our technologies focus on communication? We have no excuse for drifting apart when we have so many ways to connect.

No one is suggesting that technology could replace all face-to-face interaction all the time. What it can do is help make that interaction more valuable. If you've stayed in touch throughout the day, you don't have to waste precious evening time on errands or minor decision-making. Planning a date or a getaway is so easy online that you can actually take the time to do so—and spend more time enjoying the outing than arranging it.

And let's not forget that connection and intimacy are fun. It's an obligation, but it should not be a burden, at least not all the time. My mom's favorite advice to newlyweds is to have sex no less than once every three days. "It's like a mini-vacation," she says.

Talking About the Revolution

Come to the forums at www.reginalynn.com to share your thoughts on living solo and living together in the digital age.

Have your ideas about being single, committed or married changed because of technology?

How do you incorporate technology in your day-to-day life with your partner?

What suggestions would you give to other couples about technology's role in a relationship?

REVOLUTIONARY PROFILE
Marilyn Vokler

Marilyn K. Volker, Ed.D., has been a sexologist for almost 30 years. She is on the faculty of five universities in South Florida—University of Miami, Barry University, Florida International University, St. Thomas University and Lynn University in Boca Raton, Florida. She teaches doctors, nurses, teachers, counselors and the United States Navy and Air Force about sexuality issues and HIV/AIDS issues.

How has technology helped couples foster intimacy in their relationships?

Lots of ways! Biologically, we have Viagra, Levitra, Cialis. Procter & Gamble is going through the final FDA approvals for the Intrinsa patch for women, to help women boost their libidos. We're working on male birth control other than condoms. I've seen a wide range of people for whom fertility treatments have made a huge difference in their sex lives.

We're developing microbicides to help contain the spread of sexually transmitted diseases.

Computers have been wonderful as aids and assistants, increasing desire and sharing fantasies. So have adult films.

A lot of people go into sexuality stores now who wouldn't have before. I think there's a playfulness about it now—it isn't about being "dysfunctional." Looking at sex toys on the internet and television and radio have made it normal. We want to have accoutrements! We have sexual aids that help people with disabilities and people whose conditions aren't even that extreme—tennis elbow, rotator cuff injuries, arthritis in the hands.

We have the ability now with high tech to help people make some shifts and still remain in a relationship. For example, intersexed people—we're learning that we're not just male and female but also intersexed—can take hormones to bump up their feminine side without having to go through a sex change operation. I've seen men and women who have shifted to a more "in between" gender with their partners. Or a woman might take hormones to make intercourse easier.

I always talk about moderation, though. You have to ask questions with any drug, whether a pharmaceutical or a club drug. What's in it? And what's it going to do to my public and private parts?

Does anyone ever respond badly to a suggestion about using a vibrator or other sex aid?

When people say that these things aren't natural, I remind them that pushup bras aren't natural. Neither are eyeglasses or trimming mustaches.

How has technology changed our concepts of what a relationship is?

So many people have met successfully on the internet. We used to say oh, be careful, you never know who they really are. That's true, but that's true for meeting anyone. How they present themselves may not be what the real story is.

But I'll tell you this. My husband and I went to Hawaii last year. Hawaii is this huge honeymoon place, and we had such a great time island hopping and talking to honeymooners. A good 90 percent of them had met on the internet. These were mostly young people, our children's age, that was interesting—and great—to see.

We've been together 25 years, and there wasn't such a thing as the internet when we were meeting each other. How wonderful that people are able to meet, and if they're honest and sort through and see what happens with a relationship, they don't always have to go through the agony and money and the dating in a traditional way.

Are relationships that started online different from traditional relationships?

Internet relationships can often have a particular ebb and flow. First, there's that high spike of fantasy. If you stick with it and stay with it, it goes through its own pattern. The internet has certainly helped people find each other that they might never have found.

You still have to see if you want to work on a relationship with one another. That's the tricky part. All relationships have some element of work. No relationship maintains the high state of fantasy forever. Our bodies don't even do that—we either crash or we need Xanax. When that high level of fantasy fades is when a lot of people think "that's the end, we have to break up." But a person who knows and understands relationships says "okay, we have to be creative now."

In my job I see a lot of people willing to work on these things. I've learned a lot. People are creative. They can take the tech and evaluate: What do I want to keep doing?

9

Sex Toys:
The Play's the Thing

One of the most common questions I get from Sex Drive readers, even though I am not an advice columnist, is "How do I get my [spouse, girlfriend, boyfriend, knitting club] to let me use sex toys with them?"

If you're a toy fan and have an adventurous spirit when it comes to trying new things, you might find this hard to believe, but some—many—people find it difficult to accept sex toys into their bedrooms. These people are often intelligent, well-rounded, educated people who look just like you and me. If you passed them on the street, you'd never know that they recoil at the thought of their wives wielding dildos, or worry that their husbands will prefer the pumping, vibrating Power Stroker to them.

This concern about competition, coupled with the typical American embarrassment about sex, understandably makes us wary about bringing the more explicit aspects of sex-tech into the bedroom. Even the euphemism "marital aid" makes it sound like toys are only for use when something is wrong with your sex life.

But nothing could be further from the truth.

Sex educators generally agree that the more sex you have, the more sex you want, and the variety and sensations that sex toys can add to your sex life can keep a long-term relationship from going stale. And the internet has changed our approach to sex toys in ways the first sexual revolution did not.

You don't have to drive to Ernie's Erotic Emporium to choose one of three day-glo phalluses the size of your thigh. Instead you can log onto any number of websites that not only sell toys, they teach you how to use them. They also recommend various toys for various preferences, and in general provide a pleasant and private shopping experience that you can enjoy alone or with a partner. Who cares if the mailman suspects what's inside that plain brown wrapper? Unless you're planning to use it with him or her, it's none of his or her business what you ordered.

I think sex toys have come out of the closet for a number of reasons. One, they have become much easier to learn about and buy online. Two, the sexual adventurousness you develop after exploring online porn or cybersex makes toys seem more appealing, or even necessary, in your offline sex life. (And they solve that problem of trying to type one-handed.) Three, we feel anxious that if we don't keep up with bedroom technology, we won't be able to compete with whatever our lovers might be finding online.

That, and the Rabbit Pearl episode of "Sex and the City."

I know my expectations have changed. I used to save sex toys for solo use, figuring that it was important to have something that was just for me, not connected to anybody else. And when I wasn't in a committed relationship, I thought it would be weird to bring out sex toys, because what if the man thought I was using the same toys with other people too? I didn't want to get into any discussions about where or how or with whom I used my toys, so I kept them hidden.

These days, I have toys scattered throughout the bedroom and my home office. Partly this is because of my job—companies occasionally send me toys in hopes that I will review them. I've been known to strap on a butterfly vibe when writing about porn for my column; it helps me stay focused. But mostly, toys no longer have a stigma attached to them, nor do I feel like they need to remain secret. I, like many internet users, have become accustomed to the idea of bringing toys to bed (or wherever). Because really, after spending time at Fucking-Machines.com, it's hard to worry too much about a simple vibrator.

Starter Sex-Tech

According to a 2004 "Primetime Live" survey of American sex lives, "people who call themselves adventurous sexually are 10 points more apt to be very satisfied with their sex lives, 20 points more apt to enjoy sex a great deal and nearly 30 points more apt to call their sex lives very exciting." They're also much more likely to have sex at least several times a week—62 percent of the adventurous do so, compared with 36 percent of sexual traditionalists.

I think it's common for humans to greet new technologies with trepidation. But video didn't kill the radio star, and peer-to-peer file sharing has not put any huge music labels out of business. And vibrators are not about to replace good old sex involving penises and vaginas. Anyway, vibrators aren't really new—the first mechanical stimulators came out in the late 1800s, powered by steam. They were a medical device invented to make doctors' lives easier by automating clitoral manipulation. Before the devices, doctors had to massage women's genitals by hand until the patients reached "paroxysm" and recovered from their "hysteria." (Hysteria is a pretend disease that's been around for at least 2,000 years; I imagine that before vibrators, many a doctor risked carpal-tunnel syndrome from all that hands-on treatment.)

In fact, respectable magazines in the early 1900s carried advertisements suggesting that if you bought your wife a particular device, it would keep her looking youthful and pretty. Then stag films of the 1920s revealed the sexual nature of vibrators and forced the toys underground. It wasn't until the 1970s that stores like Good Vibrations started to revive mainstream interest in sex toys. Even though vibrators date from Victorian times, they feel new now because of the resurgence of interest and respectability surrounding them. That and the advances made in power, convenience, and performance show that vibrators are definitely part of the revolution.

One of the best ways to introduce a partner to sex toys is to start with something familiar. Niki Khanna, publicity assistant at Good Vibrations, suggests using cultural references. Saying, "I saw something on TV we could try," is a non-threatening way to broach the subject, particularly if you mention a mainstream show like "Sex and the City" (rather than late-night Spice channel porn, for example).

At press time, Good Vibrations offered three toy kits for beginners: Tools of the Trade, Jill Off and Naughty Newbies. Each kit costs less than $30 and includes a vibrator, lube and an instruction book that includes a section on using toys with your partner. That's important, Niki says, because the most common worry men have about sex toys is that the toys are intended to replace them.

"But it's not," she says. "It's just adding to what you already have." In the same way that a telephone lets you talk over distances you can't talk over without the technology, a sex toy enhances your natural abilities to give and receive sexual pleasure. Most people do not fall in love with a body part. They fall in love—or at least want to have sex with—an entire person. Anyone who would replace you with a toy isn't someone you want to be with anyway!

My recommendation for beginners is to choose toys that don't look like they're trying to be a penis or vagina. The Fukuoko 9000 (which has its own infomercial at http://asseencentral.com/fukuoko-massager.htm) is particularly suited to couples, as these small "massagers" slip onto a fingertip and provide quiet yet definite sensation. It's also discreet enough to introduce into sex with someone new—it's not as if you're whipping out 12 inches of Dr. Dong with the guy you just brought home from dance lessons. If you want more, invest in the wrist power pack, which enables you to wear three fingertip Fukuokos at a time, or the Fukuoko Five Finger Fantasy Massage Glove.

Sue Johanson's line of vibrators come in fun colors and look nothing like prosthetic penises. Candida Royalle's "Natural Contours" vibrators look like museum sculptures and will not make your boyfriend worry that there's another penis in the room. Not that there's anything wrong with another penis in the room, but part of a healthy sex life is respecting your partners' boundaries. Japanese-style vibrators tend to have cute animal shapes, like bunnies and beavers, while your local drug store probably stocks a number of personal massagers from Hitachi and Dr. Scholl's.

You don't have to limit sex toys to actual sex, either. I've had fun with the VibraExciter, which is a vibrating bullet that responds to radio frequencies. You clip the receiver onto your waistband and put the bullet wherever you like, and whenever a nearby cell phone receives or sends a signal, the bullet vibrates. This phone doesn't have to be yours, which could make for an interesting party experience. I have never managed to position it in exactly the right place for true stimulation and the vibrations aren't strong enough for me, but that's not the point. The point is that you're wearing a vibrator in public and you never know when it's going to start buzzing. Hot!

What happens if your lover agrees to try using a toy with you, and the experience isn't as smooth as you'd hoped? Have patience. Niki cautions that "the first toy you get is probably not going to be your favorite toy ever. But it will teach you what you like and don't like, so next time around you can get a toy that's better suited to your needs."

Sex toys are everywhere, even in Alabama where it's illegal to sell them (more on that in a moment). Passion Parties are giving Tupperware a run for its money—and they're mainstream enough to be written up in *O: The Oprah Magazine*. (Be honest. If you're going to attend an in-person infomercial at a friend's house, what would you rather see? Objects that burp or objects that buzz?) If even Oprah is willing to talk publicly about vibrators, you know that our cultural ideas have changed. Thanks, internet.

Do You Have a Prescription for That, Ma'am?

I have tendonitis in both arms, a chronic condition that causes me quite a bit of pain if I'm not careful. I use various devices to help me work around it, including a wireless curved keyboard and an ergonomic mouse that I can use with either hand. If I have a bad flare-up I stay off the keys for a day or two and hire my sister to type for me.

And I never masturbate by hand anymore.

I can't. It only takes about 30 seconds for the pain to shoot from my fingers to my elbow and sometimes to my shoulder. And while sex with my boyfriend is wonderful, sometimes a girl just wants to be alone, you know?

It makes me wonder what I would do if I lived in Alabama, one of the few remaining states whose obscenity law makes it illegal to "produce, distribute or otherwise sell sexual devices that are marketed primarily for the stimulation of human genital organs."

Sherri Williams, owner of upscale sexuality boutiques Pleasures I and Pleasures II and plaintiff in Williams v. Alabama, has been fighting the law since its inception in 1998. (The Supreme Court refused to hear her appeal in February 2005.) However, even this law recognizes that sex toys are not inherently criminal. It exempts sexual devices used "for a bona fide medical, scientific, educational, legislative, judicial or law enforcement purpose." It just isn't clear on what qualifies as "bona fide"—or who makes that decision.

"The reason they put that [exemption] in the law was so they didn't violate the rights of people who needed [these devices]," she says. "But the witnesses in our case are stating in their depositions that they physically need sexual aids," and it's not making any difference.

Sherri says that she cannot reach orgasm without help from a vibrator. Another plaintiff testifies that sexual intercourse is painful for her. Two other plaintiffs state that marital aids saved their marriages, while another—a 50-year-old woman—uses sex toys so she is not at risk for STDs.

Very few sexual aids have been recognized by the FDA as medical devices. One is the EROS Therapy, a suction cup you place on the clitoris. Another is the Ferticare, a penis stimulator designed for men with spinal cord injuries. Both are available by prescription, and may be covered by your insurance under insurance reimburse-ment code L7900.

The problem is that even with this particular type of sex aid—and I can tell you right now that a suction cup doesn't do anything for me—not everyone can use them easily. The Ferticare has to be held in place during use, while the EROS Therapy requires fine motor skills to apply. It seems an awfully limited selection for the esti-mated 807,000 Alabamans who have a disability.

Cory Silverberg, a sex educator and co-author of *The Ultimate Guide to Sex and Disability*, says that unfortu-nately, "sex is not considered an activity of daily living" when it comes to attendant care for people with disabili-ties. "It is illegal for a caregiver to refuse to cook a meal," he says, or to perform other intimate services such as help with toileting and bathing. "Yet (an attendant) can refuse to put a condom on someone who wants to have sex with his partner."

Cory co-owns Come As You Are, a sex store in Toronto that caters to people with disabilities as well as to the non-disabled. In the course of his work, he fields a lot of ques-tions about how technology can help someone overcome physical and emotional obstacles to sex. "The trick is to match the tech to the need," he says. It's better to adapt the toy to the person than force the person to adapt to the toy.

Replacing a dial on a vibrator with a pressure switch or a slider bar makes it more accessible to folks who lack fine motor control. You can glue a stick onto a slider to help extend a person's reach. For those who experience tremors or seizures, a butterfly vibrator—the kind held onto the body with straps—eliminates the need to hold the device in place. A bullet vibrator on a long wand helps people who cannot reach their genitals. One woman who experiences hypersensitivity as a side-effect of her medication uses a sleeve vibrator on her forearm.

Mechanics aren't the only issue. "Part of what we end up doing is increasing someone's privacy," Cory says. This is especially important for people living in group homes or who have round-the-clock attendant care. "With the right toy, someone can put it on you and leave the room."

If you aren't disabled or with a disabled partner, it might never have occurred to you how important adaptive technology is for sex as well as other aspects of daily life. Yet you don't have to have a disability to appreciate the role of tools in your sex life. Vibrators are a boon for people who type a lot; dildos can make it possible to play with various styles of penetration without the emotional consequences of a *menage a trois*.

The State of Sex Toys

Never go to Las Vegas during the first week of January unless you absolutely must. With the annual Consumer Electronics Show and two adult entertainment conventions in town, the entire Strip is packed. Between 5 and 7 p.m., it can take more than an hour just to board the monorail, where you are 90,000 times more likely to be crushed to death by engineers than by porn stars. You'll wait at least two hours to get into a restaurant if you didn't make reservations in advance and—worst of all—some hotels jack up prices on in-room broadband.

Entering the Adult Entertainment Expo 2005, I couldn't help but ogle the gigantic high-definition screen overhead and its scenes from *The Story of J*, the first adult feature shot entirely in HD. This is a film based on the groundbreaking erotic novel *The Story of O*, and features impressive production values, a beautiful cast, a female director and a plot. It's quite lovely, actually—you can probably find the trailer at DigitalPlayground.com.

The expo serves a dual purpose. On one hand, it brings together all the business people in the adult industry to make deals, sign contracts and stock their stores. On the other, it is a fan convention where porn aficionados get to meet the entertainers in person. If you push your way through the drooling fanboys and duck around the ex-linebackers guarding the girls as they pose for pictures and sign autographs, you'll find the smaller, independent exhibitors displaying their wares. It's in here that you find the true gems, products that real people use for real sex—a refreshing contrast to the studio booths up front.

This is where Sue Johanson, the "sex grandma" who hosts "Talk Sex" on Oxygen TV, introduced her line of sex toys. It is where Atraw Ceramics first displayed its line of beautiful, hand-sculpted dildos. And it is where inventors show off the latest developments in sexual technology.

Two aerospace engineers in love designed the Elemental Pleasures vibrators out of the same materials they used to build airplanes: anodized aluminum, austenitic stainless steel, titanium. These are high-end playthings, costing up to $600 for the titanium Le Lynx, which comes with three attachments and a beautiful velvet-lined box that locks. They seal completely, so you can use them in the bath, or boil them for sanitation. I don't mind admitting that I covet the Le Lynx. It has a substantial feel in the hand, yet isn't so heavy as to become unwieldy. It's the only sex toy I know of that comes with a year-long warranty.

Sex toy makers are finally thinking outside the pornographic packages. Some of these toys come in boxes you'd expect to find at Sephora or The Sharper Image. Toys are more practical now too, with seamless, snag-free construction and dishwasher-safe cleaning. Why now? Technology, of course. Not just the whizzbang glamour of teledildonics or cell phone vibrators, but the behind-the-scenes business process applications that are too boring for most sex columnists to write about.

And it's the technology that makes it possible for women to take charge, to speak out about what we want while remaining anonymous, to browse through online stores in complete privacy. It's the technology that makes it possible for a man to browse through sex toy catalogs online and find something his wife will love. Why suffer through a roadside sex shop when you can find something as beautiful as it is functional online? And if you can't find it, why not make it yourself? Even if it's a specialized niche, you'll find your market.

Why Toys Matter

Sex toys have been around as long as sex, but we are enjoying a renaissance in how we think about sexual aids. In part, we're setting aside our shame about toys and replacing it with shame about online porn or cybersex. But mainly I think we're getting a lot more comfortable talking about sex as if it were any other topic. Not with a nod to how "dirty" it is, or with a clinical perspective to make it "okay."

Toys are particularly important in cybersex when you need both hands free to type. They make webcam sex more exciting. Hook a toy up to the Sinulator and you've just added back some intimacy into your long-distance relationship (see the Cybersex chapter for more details). Include a vibrator with phone sex and your traveling partner will do everything possible to call you more often. Viagra is great at getting the parts ready but it doesn't do much for desire—adding pair of His and Hers vibrators can get both of you in the mood to do things that no 20-year-old has thought of yet.

Talking About the Revolution

Come to ReginaLynn.com to talk about sex toys in the forum.

Have you brought toys into your sex life?
Have you ever thought about creating your own sex toys?
What was your first experience with a sex toy?

REVOLUTIONARY PROFILE
Kim Airs

Kim Airs is the Proprietrix of Grand Opening, a sexuality boutique with locations in Boston and West Hollywood. We met at the Adult Entertainment Expo 2005, where she gave my companion and me an enthusiastic demonstration of how to use a thigh harness to hold a dildo in place. Grand Opening offers a full schedule of classes and demonstrations to complement the toys, games and other sexual accoutrements in the catalog.

What is the most popular item at Grand Opening?

In general, vibrators. For battery models, definitely the Japanese rabbit pearl (not an inferior knock off). Also the Hitachi Magic Wand, which is formerly Japanese but now made in China.

Any advice for someone who wants to bring toys into sex play but whose partner resists?

Introduce them as massagers, on the body, not on the genitals. And introduce it during an honest-to-Pete massage. That will get the body used to the sensation of vibration, when perhaps your partner wasn't used to it before. The Hitachi Magic Wand is good for this, as it is basically a muscle massager. Or you can use a toy that's easy to use sexually afterwards. A little pearl vibrator tucked into the palm of the hand is a great way to introduce sex toys. Make sure it's something generally regarded as non-threatening—don't walk in with twelve inches of Leroy Super Special, yelling "Hey honey, I got you a vibrator!"

Can a vibrator replace a man?

I think when men are exposed more to the benefits of vibrators, they don't fear them anymore. They realize that it will keep sex going on longer, or that now they'll get to watch their girlfriend use it. That can definitely change the attitude of both partners. A lot of it now is media-driven. When they hear Howard Stern say it's great to watch a chick use a vibrator, it gives them permission to buy one for her, instead of thinking "Oh, man, she's getting one to replace me."

Have sex toys become more acceptable, come out of the closet, since the internet?

Absolutely. The internet has a lot to do with it, but also it's generational. Today's kids have parents who grew up in the '60s and '70s when a vibrator wasn't considered that weird. So each generation is peeling the layers back. And definitely the internet has a lot to do with that.

Have sex toys changed in recent years?

I've had Grand Opening for more than 11 years now. The quality and the materials—and the sizes and sounds—have all changed significantly within the past five or six years. Why? Because the customers are demanding it. This ain't your daddy's porno anymore. We're demanding toys that are of higher quality, and because this is a consumer-driven industry, the manufacturers are responding to it. We're seeing a lot of remote controls, cordless models, more comfortable materials like silicon instead of hard plastic.

What is your personal favorite?

It depends on my mood. I actually named one "Kim's Fave"—you can see it on the website. It's pretty basic, pink jelly rubber, about eight inches long with variable speeds. I use it to get the job done. I love the size, I love the vibrations, I love the texture. It's the one that I love. And it's only $25.95! But I don't make any guarantees that everyone else will love it. Although we do sell a lot of them ...

10

Breaking Up:
Eternal Sunshine of
the Spotless Hard Drive

Whenever you have people falling in love—or at least sleeping together—you also have broken hearts, and the sexual revolution 2.0 hasn't put an end to that. In fact, it has fueled more heartbreak than it probably needs to. Yet even heartbreak is not what it once was.

We're no longer separated by a comfortable six degrees; the internet can eliminate several intermediaries with a single Google search. It's likely that the love we've just lost will still be in our social circle, online or off. Or, when we most want our exes to disappear, they continue to pop up at the least convenient times. How much of your relationship is on your hard drive, saved and searchable?

Part of our task in the next several years is to adapt our expectations about how relationships end, if they are to end, and how to handle the ramifications of an era where we can jilt or be jilted from a distance.

In Malaysia, where, according to a friend of mine who lives there, *everyone* is addicted to SMS, the courts ruled it legal to divorce your wife through text messaging, although even the judge agreed it was more polite to do it with a phone call. (A Muslim man can divorce his wife by telling her three times, "I divorce you.") Compared to that, maybe getting dumped by a lover through email is not quite so shocking.

Yet despite the relaxation of the stigma that used to apply to meeting or falling in love online, America has yet to become comfortable with the idea of breaking up online. Thank you notes and sympathy cards must still be written by hand and mailed, while breaking up is supposed to take place in person. Or at the very least, in a phone call.

We'll Always Have ICQ

I used to have a friend who lived on the other side of the world.

I say a friend, but in the seven years of our relationship, we had been many things to one another—online buddies, editorial partners, offline friends, realspace lovers—although not all at the same time.

For the first five years we lived a mere 2,000 miles apart. When he moved, very little changed for us, as the vast majority of our interaction took place online anyway. (In seven years, we spent about 60 days together in person.) We adjusted to the new time zone, chatting in the mornings and evenings when our schedules overlapped.

But as my work became more demanding and he began to travel to more remote and spiritual destinations, our friendship began to change. I talked about writing this book and how I'd underestimated the time it was taking to pull it all together. He talked about his deepening under-standing of Eastern culture—and, by contrast, Western.

As he began to eschew material things, I struggled to put a down payment on a house small enough to fit into my previous apartment. As he talked about showing me the temples and sacred places of Southeast Asia, I talked about increasing my hours at my day job and finding a roommate so I could make my mortgage payments.

Our conversations became less frequent, and when we did chat, I felt strained and unsure. For the first time, we had to work to find common ground. We talked about my coming to visit and how I would work on my book while I was there. We said how excited we were at the prospect of seeing each other again. And we kept any misgivings to ourselves.

One week before my departure, it became clear to me that I would have to choose between my professional obli-gation to finish my book, which was already two months overdue, or my personal commitment to go on the trip and fall another month behind.

If I went and worked, I would wonder why I had traveled so far just to sit at my computer. If I didn't work, I wouldn't be able to engage with the wonders around me because I'd be stressing about the book.

I canceled the trip. I emailed my decision to my friend and waited for the fallout. I knew he would be disap-pointed and exasperated, maybe angry, and I found I was nervous about his reply.

I need not have been. It never came.

I've read a lot over the years about internet relation-ships. I've perused the studies, heard the anecdotes, par-ticipated in discussions about this new frontier in human sexuality and interpersonal connection.

It has almost become mainstream to start relationships on the internet. Dr. Marilyn Volker estimates that 90 percent of the newlyweds she talked to on her Hawaiian vacation—and there were a lot—said they met online. Meanwhile, single people never have to stay home alone on a Saturday night if they are willing to travel and keep their standards . . . flexible.

Yet when it comes to breaking up, there's not much out there to help you figure out what to do.

Most of us know how to jilt someone offline. You have a conversation in person, one or both of you cries, someone's heart breaks (or not), and you piece your life back together one step at a time.

But the internet has facilitated so many more types of relationships that it's hard to know what to do when things go wrong. We have friendships that stay online, friendships that cross from online to off and back again, and friendships that start offline but migrate to cyberspace.

There's the cyber lover who gives you the best orgasm of your life, the cyber lovers you keep secret from your other cyber lovers, and the cyber lover who knows all about your partner but begs to meet you in person anyway. There's the Match.com girl you dated three times and have no interest in seeing again. There's the guy who keeps emailing you long after he should have given up.

What is the etiquette for ending these non-traditional arrangements? Do three dates with someone you met online obligate you to a breakup phone call? Or is email enough? If you had a cybersex relationship so hot your computer almost caught fire, do you owe your virtual paramour an explanation if you decide to quit cybering after a week?

I met my friend on the internet. It's the platform that held us together all those years, and the place where we felt we most understood one another. We marveled at how we had found such a true meeting of the minds and spent more time together than with anyone else, online or off.

But in the end, even we didn't break up there.

When I didn't get a reply email or see him on IM for a week, I followed up with a phone call, on the slim chance that my messages had gone astray. That's when I learned I had offended him so deeply that as far as he was concerned, our friendship was over. He didn't explain why, and after several minutes of silence, I hung up.

For a while I expected to receive an email with an explanation. Without it, I can only assume he felt I was choosing work over friendship, which had been a sticking point for us in the past. And I realize now just how easy it is to break up online.

I've always championed the legitimacy of online relationships. It may be "on the internet," but that's still a real person on the other side of the chat. Over seven years of almost daily IMing, I was as close to this friend as I've ever been with anyone. Yet neither of us had to walk away, close a door, drive home. Neither of us had to see the look on each other's faces, or cope with tears or the inability to meet each other's eyes.

He didn't have to worry about me barging into his apartment and demanding to know why. If I wasn't going to wait on the line, paying international long distance until he decided to talk, he couldn't keep me there with a gesture or a look.

It takes two minutes to remove someone from your IM lists, even if that person has eight handles across five different clients. You can filter incoming emails straight to trash if you don't want to deal with someone again. You don't run into your online exes around town.

Online relationships tend to be emotional, because that's the kind of connection we make when we remove the physical from the equation. But without the physical reminders that someone has left behind -- a shared table at the local café, the friends you hung out with together, a toothbrush -- it's a hell of a lot easier to get through the emotional upheaval and move on with your life.

And I don't really know how I feel about that yet.

50 Ways to Delete Your Lover

Breaking up is different now because dating and relationships are different now. Online dating catalogs still contain pages describing people you've already returned, or who returned you. Forums, discussion groups, blogs, listservs—if you met through any sort of online community, your history is still in the archives. Email, instant messaging and blog comments do not disappear just because a couple breaks up. You can't just stuff it in the attic or toss it on the fireplace—there's an entire process to eliminating the digital detritus of a relationship gone sour.

One my most popular columns was the one in which I outlined how my temporary boyfriend had insinuated himself on my computer and the virtual acrobatics I performed to erase his artifacts from my hard drive, if not his memory from my mind. I heard from people whose friends had forwarded the column to them. I was interviewed by *The New York Times*. It seems that column touched something deep and familiar for many, many people.

What happened was, I was searching my for the combination to my bike lock, which I knew I had emailed to a friend. Yet what popped up first was not the six digits I needed but rather an email from the English professor I had dated in what turned out to be the most embarrassing—and the briefest—romantic relationship I've had. Our relationship would have ended soon anyway, but as it happened, the end came when the prof admitted he was sleeping with a student. The student, a 44-year-old whose "day job" was being the mistress of a billionaire, had no intention of leaving her cushy situation for the prof's modest salary.

Now I understand why Dave Barry has to pause sometimes to reassure readers that he is not making this up.

The real kicker, though, is that I was experimenting with monogamy again after a few years of polyandrous dating. And the reason I did *that* was that the professor seduced me so thoroughly by email and IM. By the time he met me in person and declared it was exclusivity or nothing, I decided what the hell, I'd try going steady.

Within three months, I suspected his affair but chose not to ask him about it for reasons I can't remember now. The holidays were approaching and I would be taking care of his dog while he left town to visit family. I figured that upon his return I would inquire, and we would re-negotiate our arrangement—either go poly, or part ways altogether. That conversation turned into a blubbering, weeping almost-confession on his part and a curious lack of feeling on mine.

When I do something, I can't do it halfway unless it's housework (in which case the challenge is to get through at least half). When I ended things for real, I did it 100 percent: no phone, no email, no IM, not even a "Sorry, Charlie." I went through my computers and cleared off everything I could find. His screenplay, his erotica, his pictures, IM logs, email. I created filters to comb through my Inbox and Outbox, to intercept incoming mail, and send all his missives straight to the trash. It wasn't that I hated him, but I knew I'd be tempted to read the mail, which would not help me put that brief-but-intense relationship behind me. It's that naked email thing again—nothing more dangerous than a Mr. Wrong who writes like Mr. Right Now.

I didn't set up my filters well enough. They only searched the To and From fields. And in looking for a bike lock combo, I found an email that had his address in the CC field.

It's one thing to bask in the technostalgia of tender love letters from someone you think fondly of, or to run across an IM log in which you cowrote a ridiculous country song with a new special friend. It's another to have the biggest relationship mistake of your life popping up during innocent searches.

10 Steps to a Spotless Hard Drive

But as the song says, there must be 50 ways to delete your lover. And if you don't do all of them, your technology may bring him or her back to haunt you.

1. Block every IM handle they gave you.

2. Set your IM client to accept messages only from people already on your buddy list.

3. Remove them from your contact list so you don't make yourself crazy monitoring their online habits.

4. Destroy all email both from and to them, checking the CC and BCC fields as well.

5. If they know about your online dating profile, see whether you can block them from viewing it or contacting you. (Some sites don't have this feature, alas.)

6. Check My Pictures, My Documents and your attachments folder for images to send to the recycle bin.

7. Delete their email addresses from your address books, and don't forget to check any group nicknames that might include them.

8. Delete their contact information from your PDA, your text-messaging device and your cellphone.

9. Delete links from your blog, online journal and social networking profiles that point to them.

10. Consider leaving email discussion lists and web forums where you might run into them.

How Long Is Your Digital Trail?

I sometimes think about what I've left behind on other computers. How many of my emails linger in archives in Seattle, San Francisco, the South? Did the prof save any of our correspondence? He likes drama, he would seek the delicious ache of past love, especially when the affair with the billionaire's mistress fell apart.

I have kept some beautiful email I've received over the years, and pictures, too—not the kind you can show your friends when they ask you what your lover looks like. I have sent some of those types of pictures out as well. All I can do is trust that the recipients keep them as private as I keep theirs. Some of my friends and exes might still have rough drafts of smut from when I considered writing porn ("I never believed these stories were true, but . . .").

I can't help but laugh when I think about the IM logs that might still exist. Like most people, I'm hardly circumspect during late-night chats. I once built an entire gothic novella with an internet lover simply by typing words and short phrases into ICQ. It would read ridiculously now, but caught up in the moment we were both so turned on that I wish I still had the transcript. (This eternal sunshine thing works both ways; a tech disaster can erase artifacts you would rather have kept, so do what your IT department is always telling you to do and *back up your data*.)

I would rather write from the heart and risk regretting what I have revealed than be afraid to express myself, even if that means I leave a digital trail that could come back to haunt me in the future. What I say is honest and true at the moment I say it, so how could that be bad?

When I was writing the Cybersex chapter, I paused to reflect upon what being Aphrodite has meant in my life. That in turn led to my wondering what had happened to a few people, one in particular, which of course led me to Google.

The problem with Google, computers, the whole internet shebang is that it's all right there, all the time, even at 2:00 a.m. when your judgment is impaired by nostalgia and tiredness and maybe a glass of wine and a sentimental novel. And because it's right there, it's hard to resist its lure, especially if you have Wi-Fi and you don't even have to get out of bed to look somebody up.

Here's what happened: I had a love affair with a man who lived across the country. It started in the chat room, moved to the telephone and graduated to the real world whenever we could afford a plane ticket. Still, most of our interaction occurred through the miracles of technology. (And now you know why I can't bring myself to throw away that busted old webcam. Ah, memories.)

Eventually, it became clear that neither of us was going to move across the country permanently, and we agreed to stop being lovers so we (read: he) could focus on developing a local relationship. He met someone a few months later, and then the new girlfriend asked him to cut off all communication with me. After the longest phone call of my life (seven hours!), in which we tried to say everything we'd ever need to say, communication ceased. I respected his decision and his dedication to his new relationship, and I have not called or written since. (I did send his Christmas present soon after our conversation, because that pre-dated The End, and what was I going to do with a second copy of the entire Lyle Lovett library?)

Conversation may have ended—or been postponed 20 years, you never know, it's so easy to get back in touch with people these days—but curiosity didn't. Every now and then, in a weak moment, I search, although it's been almost five years since that last conversation. I look for hometown news about him, his son, his mother who had been ill; and I never found anything until recently, when I discovered he'd put his band back together and released an album.

What can I say? It was after midnight. If one truly wants to honor the spirit of a breakup, one does not spend time online after midnight. I ordered the album.

I ordered it knowing the band had recorded it themselves to sell at regional shows, that I had met one of the other band members in person, and that my Los Angeles address was going to be noticed. When one band member e-mailed me to confirm my address, I did so, and after listening to the record I sent him another note telling him how much I enjoyed it. But my ex did not contact me, and I left it at that.

In just the past few years, it's become harder than ever to avoid leaving a digital trail. Gone are the days when you had to make an effort to be on the web. Now, you have to work to stay off it.

If you make your local paper, it doesn't matter if the paper doesn't archive its past issues—Google's cached pages will do it for you. Your friends blog you, your listservs archive your posts, and online phone directories have your number. Your band gets popular and someone starts a fan site. Or someone reviews a festival at which the band played, and your whereabouts are "outed" for all your exes to see.

Run your own business? You're online, and your past can find you. Start a wish list—or a wedding registry—on a retailer's website? You're online, and your past can find you. If you do anything at all that brings you in contact with the public, whether it's a band gig or a volunteer day with a local charity or getting arrested or writing a blurb in the corporate newsletter, your name is as likely to appear online as not. And if you really want to risk having 10 years of participation in the sexual revolution 2.0 exposed, write a book in which your old internet gang might recognize themselves despite changes of name and other details that might identify them to others.

It was not hard to find my former swain. A simple Google search brought up the band website, reviews in area press and listings of events where the band will be playing over the holidays. We're not talking about U2 here, just a medium fish in a small pond, and yet he's as easy to find as any mega star.

An ex used to think twice before approaching you, because anything she did to you might rebound onto her. In small towns especially, any public action—even one as innocuous as her speaking to your new girlfriend at a community event—can have consequences for all parties concerned.

But the internet negates those consequences. One of the major changes the sexual revolution 2.0 has wrought is the ease with which we can get involved with each other across state and international borders. That means there are often no local community standards to stop us from post-breakup shenanigans. We can harass each other without the neighbors knowing, and we can exact revenge simply by attaching a compromising photo to an e-mail sent to the last person on the planet who should see it. We can even act with all the intensity of a jilted inamorato after just one date, or one flirtatious chat.

Even the most well-meaning, upstanding citizen might have a different understanding than you do about the boundaries you each think you've set for your breakup. I know I violated the spirit, if not the letter, of the cease-contact agreement by ordering that album. Even though I made no effort to email him directly, and I can't bring myself to regret the purchase, as it's a great album, I'm not comfortable with my own rationalization. And yet I'm listening to the album right now to inspire me as I write this section.

One of my deepest-held beliefs about sex in the information age is that we all must develop a deeper respect for each other's privacy. An honor system, if you will, where we do not seek vengeance online, we do our best not succumb to the temptation of the midnight e-mail, and we do not post fierce comments in our exes' blogs when they start writing about their new lovers. Yet I cannot expect us all to uphold our dignity in every single circumstance. When our hearts are involved, it's impossible to be strong all of the time.

We intersect with each other now in so many protocols, it's only fair that we develop an etiquette that helps us all maintain our dignity—no matter which side of the breakup we're on. It means that to take advantage of all that the sexual revolution 2.0 has to offer us, we have to become more mature in how we handle the painful events and those involved in them.

198 THE SEXUAL REVOLUTION 2.0

Divorce, Dissolution and Disillusion

Most of us come into contact with many more people in any given day than previous generations did. With women and men both working in corporate settings, we have many more chances to spend significant amounts of time with people other than our partners. The long hours and all-but-mandatory social events many jobs require mean we may be interacting more frequently with workmates than lovers. How can you help but form bonds with the attractive, intelligent people with whom you are thrown together? Especially if that person understands what you're going through, what your job requires of you, and you feel your mate doesn't.

Newsweek reported in 2004 that American wives were just as likely as husbands nowadays to have affairs, and basically blamed the internet for the increase in female infidelity. It might be nice to think the answer is so simple, but complicated factors like opportunity, sexual confidence, and emotional vulnerability contribute just as much to this social change. It's also possible that women feel more comfortable reporting their indiscretions in surveys than they did in the past. Yet the internet certainly makes it easier to manage the logistics of an affair. And all of the examples in this book of how tech can help us nurture our relationships apply to affairs, too.

Cybersex, whether complex mutual masturbation involving power tools and a camera crew or just simple flirting, can make a real-world affair seem much more possible than it did before you started chatting. The temptation inherent to meeting a vast number of people who want you, the catalog mentality perpetuated by online dating, and the opening up of our sexual discussions and expectations, all combine to put pressure on couples who might otherwise have been able to resist having flings.

We have so many choices now, men and women both, it has become more difficult to stick it out through the hard times in a marriage or long-term commitment. Why put the work into it when you can just find another one? Why stay with someone who doesn't understand you as deeply, as truly, as intimately as your online "friend"?

These are questions we all have to answer for ourselves.

Why Eternal Sunshine Matters

Tech has a big impact on how our relationships end in the sexual revolution 2.0. An online affair can destroy your marriage; a series of online dating partners who didn't work out may make you feel like you're dumping people by form letter.

The reality is, most of us get our hearts broken in a big way at least once, with or without the internet. And most of us experience many relationship endings during our lifetimes. It shouldn't be a surprise in our ever-connected world that we would use technology to make it easier to say those seven dirty words: "I think we should just be friends."

Relationships themselves have changed dramatically in response to technology. Would you still be in touch with former flames if not for email? Would you have friendships with people you met for a first date but broke off with almost immediately afterward? When you categorize your relationships, how many people fall outside the spouse/co-worker/relative/friend paradigm?

I never think of ex-lovers as friends in the same way I think of my other friends as friends. With girlfriends, I hold very little back. With friends who were once lovers, current partners come up in conversation only often enough to remind each other that they exist; it seems rude to dish about current love lives, even if we've been exes for years.

I'm just waiting for someone to come out with software that will track your love affairs for you. If the relationship turns sour, you click a button to start a scan—something like a virus scan. Every email, IM log, photo, story, everything pulled up for you to glance through one last time. Then *click*, all gone. Not recycled, just gone.

After all, you still have your memories.

Talking About the Revolution

Come to the forums at www.reginalynn.com to exchange ideas about how technology plays a role in the end of a relationship.

> *How has technology changed the way you end a relationship?*
> *Do you worry about your digital trail?*
> *Is the internet to blame for any of your past breakups?*

REVOLUTIONARY PROFILE
Lynn Harris

Lynn Harris is co-creator (with Chris Kalb) of Breakup Girl, a comic strip character who helps men and women with relationship emergencies (not just breakups!). Lynn is also the author of the comic novel Miss Media (iUniverse 2003) and the founder of BreakupGirl.net, a resource for any stage of a relationship.

How is technology affecting how we break up?

While we definitely see differences in relationships now because of technology, I do think people often ascribe to technology things that might happen anyway. For example, people still don't call when they say they will call, when a relationship is fading or when they're making a point.

But now we have entirely new ways of not calling. If someone says "I tried to call you," it's always obviously a lie. How can they *try* to call you? As Yoda said, there is no try. Even if the voicemail is on the blink, you probably have an incoming call log. With email, Blackberries, cell phones and whatever else people have that I don't know about, there is no way *not* to get in touch with someone.

So the failure to reach out is a lot more resounding than it used to be.

Is it okay to break up by email, IM or text messaging?

The only time it's okay to break up by text message is if the relationship has consisted solely of text messages. The same is true of email.

But email is perfect for non-breakup breakups. If you've gone out with someone a few times and he or she is into it and you're not, to have a big breakup would be excessive. You're not boyfriend and girlfriend. If you've had two or three dates and things seemed promising but now they aren't, do you really have to see them to break up? Of course not. That would constitute 25 percent of your entire relationship.

You do have to have a conversation with that person. Call or email and be really really nice. But don't waste their time setting up a whole date just to break up. That's stupid, and it's only falsely respectful.

You did mention that email can play a role when a relationship is ending. What is appropriate?

If you had a conversation but you didn't say exactly what you wanted to say, or you couldn't respond quite the way you wanted to respond, email is a good way to follow up.

I do recommend, if you're very angry, that you don't put the person's name in the To: line at first so you don't hit send prematurely. Save the email in your drafts folder for at least 12 to 24 hours. Or send it to a friend first, and wait to see if you really want to send it to the person you're angry with.

Not that there's anything wrong with being angry. The email just might not be the way you want to put it. Still, email is good way to communicate if you're too upset or angry to see each other, but you want to talk in close to real time.

What do you think about the influence of online porn or cybersex on breaking up?

This is one area where tech creates a relationship challenge that wasn't there before. Not the fact of porn obviously, as that's been around, but the ease of getting it. You don't have to get in the car, go to the drugstore and buy something from some punk teen who's probably in your kid's class. That you don't have to do that makes an absolutely quantifiable difference.

The thing is, I don't think couples say across the board that porn hurts their relationship. When secrecy and spending inordinate amounts of time apart gets involved, that's when they get upset. When he's online, it's often not that he's looking at naked ladies, it's that he's online when she's reading *Goodnight Moon* to the kids. In many cases these aren't people who would be driving to the store to get porn.

Honestly, even though I just said the tech is creating a problem that may not have been there otherwise, I also think it indicates a problem in the relationship. It just happens to be internet porn, but it could just as well be some other easily accessible means of escape. It indicates something wrong, maybe not terribly wrong but definitely not right, with the relationship. It's a problem if there is no disincentive to turn off the computer and go read *Goodnight Moon*.

Do you think we're finding more ways to escape, rather than handle relationship issues, now that we're so high tech?

That's a good question. It's hard to say across the board. In online dating or meeting people online, there's always going to be someone who's a pro, who knows they can always go back to it and meet someone else. And there's always someone else who didn't enjoy it, who resists or even hates the idea of meeting people online.

But even technology, for better or for worse, cannot in all cases override the urge that many people have to stay with what they have and make it work. Now, staying to make it work is not by definition the virtuous thing to do. You could be in a bad relationship and on a fool's errand to try to make it work. Especially if the only reason to stay is to avoid being single again!

11

The Future of Sex

Remember the movie *Demolition Man*? Sylvester Stallone, Wesley Snipes and Sandra Bullock star in a futuristic Los Angeles setting. Sandra plays a cop of the last 21st century, while Sly plays a cop from the 1990s who was cryogenically frozen as punishment for a crime he didn't commit. When the "criminal of the century" (Wesley) thaws himself out and goes on a murderous rampage, he discovers a future rendered crime-free by a number of technologies created to control thoughts and behaviors. The cops, unable to handle the violent Wesley, revive Sly to go after him.

The plot is standard action-comedy, but what stays with you are the little details that make the future world. "Taco Bell won the franchise wars," Sandra tells us. "All restaurants are Taco Bell." The radio plays advertising jingles from the '80s and '90s. And when Sandra invites Sylvester to have sex, she quite naturally reaches for the virtual reality helmet.

It's a great scene, actually. He can't quite get the hang of the technology, and his mind instinctively resists surrendering control to their combined imaginations and the resulting sensory stimulation. She can't figure out why he keeps trying to touch her, particularly with lips (bodily fluids, ew!). The movie focuses on the humor of the situation, but the reason Sandra gives for why sex has gone virtual is serious: pandemics of STDs more serious than AIDs.

The movie beats you over the head with its message. Old-fashioned sex and violence—especially violence, because this is an all-ages film—are a better way of life for human beings than any clean-machine living. Take away bodily fluids and we lose our vitality, the animal part of us that make us superior to even the most sophisticated AI engine.

Everywhere you look, someone wants to scare you about the future. We'll all become cybersex addicts and leave our spouses. Virtual reality will replace lovemaking. We'll forget what our lovers smell like, although we'll be intimately familiar with the parts of their bodies that fit into a webcam frame. Online pornography will ensnare children, flood their tender brains with dangerous erotoxins, and warp an entire generation's sexual development with images of extreme fetishes and kinks.

I have deliberately taken a positive stance with this book because that is how I honestly see the sexual revolution 2.0. I am not oblivious to the negative effects the misuse of sexual technology can have on a person and a relationship, and I am not naive enough to blame every disastrous use of the technology on an individual's weak character. As with another major area of technological innovation—warfare—sexual technology brings with it a host of opportunities to wreak havoc, whether through succumbing to unhealthy temptations or through ignorance or arrogance.

It's why all through this book I have encouraged, urged, insisted that we pay attention. Don't let embarrass-

206 THE SEXUAL REVOLUTION 2.0

ment or fear prevent you from talking about sex or tech. You can do so anonymously online, and reginalynn.com is a safe place to start. But it's also important to bring it up in your relationships. I can't tell you how many emails I've received from readers who tell me that their wife's obsession with sexy chat has become an issue, and that they have helplessly stood by while she spent more and more time at the computer over the course of a year. Or whose husbands spend so much time looking at online porn that the reader has felt pushed out of the relationship for the past six months. Hello? Six months, a year, and you haven't said anything?

Pay attention. Talk. Be willing to be uncomfortable. Be willing to trust that your partner is not intentionally replacing you with technology. Be willing to admit that your fascination with cybersex or porn or online dating or blogging could create tension in your relationship, whether through resentment, jealousy, insecurity or all of the above. Call upon all of your skills for non-confrontational discussion. If you don't have any, consult a professional. Remember you can always use email and IM to start the conversation if you just can't bring yourself to say it aloud.

By definition, the latest tech is novel and exciting. I'm the last person who will say we shouldn't use it. If we can all learn to use it well, we can prevent all those things They are afraid of from coming to pass.

The Big Scary

I hate the thought that sexually active adults and teens find excuses to forego condoms and other accoutrements of safer sex.

I can't believe that some states outlaw various sexual devices and behaviors performed in private among consenting adults.

I think it's weird that post-menopausal women are having babies.

Every story about a CEO with a hard drive full of child porn, a teenager lured into a real-world date with an adult chat buddy, or a series of men who showed up at a house thinking they were meeting a 14-year-old for sex makes my blood boil.

I mourn for marriages broken by internet infidelity and jobs lost to obsession with cybersex or online porn— or even just a personal blog.

I loathe that people hide behind the internet so they can be rude and obnoxious without facing any significant consequences, which ruins the fun of sex-tech for the rest of us.

I wish we never had to ask questions like these:

Why is my husband obsessed with Hot Young Anal Sluts dot com?

Why is my wife spending all of her time with her cyber lover?

Why is my lover's personal ad still online after six months of exclusively dating me?

But I wish we all had the courage to ask those questions out loud, through whatever communication medium best suits us, before it's too late.

I see the fear growing among people who don't understand the technology, or who don't understand that other people having consensual sex does not hurt anyone. I see this fear lashing out in attempts to control how other people incorporate sex toys, sexual acts and sexual imagery into their private lives.

I wish we weren't developing an inferiority complex about technology and its role in our relationships. My column puts me in the unique position of hearing an underlying anxiety among technophiles and technophobes alike: *How can I compete with technology when I'm just a normal human being, complete with flaws, fears and fluids?*

You can't. Because ultimately, it's not a competition.

The Future of Sex

We use all kinds of technologies to extend our personal capabilities. We can't fly so we board planes. We can't run 80 miles per hour so we drive cars. We can't project our voices more than half a city block so we use phones. We can't remember what we promised to pick up at the store so we make lists in our PDAs (or, if we're really retro, on paper). We can't run out in the middle of a business meeting to steal a kiss from our beloved—especially if he or she is not nearby—so we send discreet text messages. All of these technologies serve to help us do something our bodies can't do on their own, but they do not replace our inherent abilities. Even in Los Angeles, we haven't stopped walking just because we can drive.

We are in charge of how we incorporate technology into sex. No technology will force us into anything, but we can master the technology that enhances our abilities and our experiences. That could mean an elaborate, long-distance sexual encounter facilitated by various electronic signals and devices. It could mean a text message hinting at the sensual delights you intend to seek out with your partner the next time you get together. It could mean a fingertip vibrator slipped between your bodies to bring additional pleasure to lovemaking.

One thing I've noticed is that we no longer question whether something can be done. Instead, we ask when we'll figure out how to do it. With so much classic science fiction already science fact, what is left to be surprised about? With sex to drive tech and tech to transform sex, I doubt the human imagination will ever reach its limit.

I asked Sex Drive readers to tell me where they thought sex and tech will come together over the next 10 to 50 years. Each suggestion seems totally possible, and has its roots in technologies available today.

Hook, a software designer in Perth, predicts "a merging of genuinely intelligent artificial intelligence and virtual reality used for a lot of purposes, particularly the creation and provision of sex partners. The VR I'm referring to is something that models the real world accurately enough to be indistinguishable, allowing total immersion. It's the ultimate in safe sex, as long as your fantasy doesn't get hacked."

Implanted chips could "electrically enhance the electro-biochemical stimulation of pleasure sites within the brain to enhance the feeling of an orgasm. A 'bionic orgasm,' if you will," writes Simon of Toronto, Canada.

An extension of that could be vibrators, dildos or artificial vaginas or breasts with a wireless link to your brain "so you can experience sensation as if the body part was real," he says. "Guys could feel like they have two penises and double-penetrate a partner. Or a woman could feel what it is like to have a penis, while a man could feel what it is like to have a vagina or breasts. Could that enhance emotional sensitivity and understanding between the sexes?"

Several people wrote about the larger effects tech might have on sexuality in our culture. "It will continue to blur the lines of fundamental concepts like gender, fidelity, privacy and beauty," writes Fred of Manassas, Virginia. He predicts a dichotomy in how we respond to these changes, with some people welcoming them and others fearful. "Since fear is a more powerful motivator than sex, the government will become more and more repressive of people who explore the new sexual territories," he says. If that's not reason enough to pay attention and keep the conversation going—and growing—I don't know what is.

One of my regular correspondents, Bob, believes that "simplicity is eventually going to win out," and that "some part of the population will simply exist outside caring about it."

And Lee, another regular, believes the future lies in innovative software running on the same type of hardware that we have today, just cleverer "or sillier." He foresees "a videophone that does photorealistic rendering to make you look 10 or 20 pounds lighter, changes your sex, changes the length or style or color of your hair, shows naked skin where really you're wearing clothes, or vice versa. And it'll do all this on the picture stream you're sending—or receiving." It's the kind of fantasy that voice changers and chat rooms let you do now, but with full immersion.

Tech can provide us with variety and novelty. It can give us more ways to share pleasure. It helps us find partners, in the spirit and in the flesh. It gives us an outlet for personal expression and mutual connection unlike anything the world has ever seen.

The future of sex is just that: sex, only better.

Dig it.

Other Books
by Ulysses Press

Sexploration: An Edgy Encyclopedia
of Everything Sexual
Suzi Godson, $16.95
This innovative and visually stunning book explores the near and far reaches of sexuality in an open-minded and adventurous style.

The Best Sex You'll Ever Have!
Richard Emerson, $12.95
Packed with a variety of new ideas to spice up lovemaking, *The Best Sex You'll Ever Have!* illustrates risque positions, fantasies, role playing, sex toys and erotic games.

The Little Bit Naughty Book of Sex
Dr. Jean Rogiere, $9.95
A handy pocket hardcover that is a fun, full-on guide to enjoying great sex.

The Little Bit Naughty Book of Sex Positions
Siobhan Kelly, $9.95
Fully illustrated with 50 tastefully explicit color photos, *The Little Bit Naughty Book of Sex Positions* provides everything readers need to start using these thrilling new positions tonight.

Naughty Girls' Night In
Shana Duthie & Stacey Jewell, $14.95
From enjoying a night of sexy fun with your girlfriends to starting a highly profitable home business, this book describes everything you need to know about in-home sex-toy parties.

Lose That Loser and Find the Right Guy: Stop Falling for Mr. Unavailable, Mr. Unreliable, Mr. Bad Boy, Mr. Needy, Mr. Married Man and Mr. Sex Maniac

Jane Matthews, $12.95

This book helps a woman identify the wrong type of man, change negative dating habits and build a relationship that is right for her.

The Sexy Bitch's Party: Living It, Throwing It and Being It

Lulu Davidson, $10.00

Gives women advice on how to set the scene, serve great food, mix fabulous drinks and seed a party with playful things that will turn ordinary guests into sexy bitch cohorts.

So You Wanna be a Sexy Bitch: Raise Your Game from Overlooked Nice Girl to Skilled Chick Everyone Wants to Get With

Flic Everett, $9.95

A Sexy Bitch isn't born, she makes herself with one thing: her attitude. This book is a road map to raising a woman's self-image in the area of life where it matters most: sex.

The Wild Guide to Sex and Loving

Siobhan Kelly, $16.95

Packed with practical, frank and sometimes downright dirty tips on how to hone your bedroom skills, this handbook tells you everything you need to know to unlock the secrets of truly tantalizing sensual play.

To order these books call 800-377-2542 or 510-601-8301, fax 510-601-8307, e-mail ulysses@ulyssespress.com, or write to Ulysses Press, P.O. Box 3440, Berkeley, CA 94703. All retail orders are shipped free of charge. California residents must include sales tax. Allow two to three weeks for delivery.

About the Author

Regina Lynn writes the popular "Sex Drive" column for Wired.com. She won the Western Publication Association's 2005 Maggie Award for Best Online Column, and she has been featured in *The New York Times*, NPR New Zealand, "Digital Village" on Radio Pacifica, and "Midnight Sex Talk" on Resonance 104.4 FM in London. Still, nothing delights her more than getting a column listed on FARK.com. Regina lives in Los Angeles with her dog, Jedi, and her fish, Squishy and Nigel. When not handcuffed to her computer, she can be found carving the canyons on her motorcycle or hanging out at the beach with inline skates and a boogie board. Her birthday is in May but she accepts presents year round.